Unknown for Over Six Decades:

The Rediscovery of Louis "Blues Boy" Jones

By LaVern Jones Lemons

MARKED UNKNOWN FOR 60 YEARS!

I especially, thank Matt Lum for the great work he's done on the book cover. It is the work of a masterpiece!

Table of Contents

Dedication
Introduction

Table of Contents

Table of Contents

Dedication

After discovering Louis Blues Boy Jones' music on the Internet, I told my sister Taneshia that I would write a book and hopefully someone would make a movie about our Dad's life someday.

I dedicate this book to some of the loves of my life: my Dad, Grandma, my Mom, my brothers Harold and Louis III, Taneshia, other family members and all of Blues Boy Jones' great followers in places worldwide! Remember...Life is a blessing, enJOY and love from deep within your heart.

INTRODUCTION

My name is LaVern Rebecca Jones Lemons. I am the oldest daughter of the late Louis Prince Jones Jr. Jones, a native of Galveston, Texas, was a blues singer during the early 1950s and 60s. My mother is Louise Frances Ford and she resides in San Francisco, California. I am married to Pastor Hollis O'Neal Lemons. I have three amazing children: two daughters and one son. I have four beautiful granddaughters and one multi-talented grandson. We reside in Clute, Texas. As a young girl, I must admit that I was fascinated when it came to my dad because I felt like there was just something special about him that I didn't know.

For many years, as young children, my two older brothers and I traveled to the breathtaking and beautiful Galveston Island to spend the summer with our grandparents. While there, our dad would come by to visit with us. These were some of the grandest moments in life for me. As a little girl, just seeing my dad meant everything in this world to me. This book will be loving, yet at times very emotional and tearful for me because I came to the realization that in our lives, some things will remain unanswered. As the story unfolds, people will be able to feel and identify with some of the same experiences perhaps in their lives, or perhaps identify with someone that they know. My dad passed away over thirty years ago, but lately his music is being viewed and purchased worldwide over the Internet.

A Special Tribute to my Brothers

Harold Leonard Jones, my dear brother, for twelve days each year, we were the same age. We laughed about this each year until he passed me up again. Back in December 2012, he was diagnosed with a rare lung cancer, stage three. Everyone to lifted him up in prayer and we were so thankful for each and every prayer. Harold resembled our Dad the most. Also, he had our dad's witty and fun-loving personality. Harold we love you; be encouraged and know my dear brother that you are never alone. We believe that by faith, God is with you and you with him. My dearest brother, I love you and I dedicate this book to you and my other siblings.

Louis Jones III was our oldest brother. He has had his fair share of life's trials and struggles. Louis we love you and know this, my dearest big brother, that with God all things are possible.

We are still striving to locate who has ownership of Louis (Blues Boy) Jones' music. We, his four children, are his legal heirs and we are seeking to claim the rights to our dad's music. Our dad left such an amazing legacy behind and I am grateful to be sharing the story of Louis "Blues Boy" Jones' life with people in locations around the world who love, respect and enjoy listening to his beautiful yet timeless music. Dad, we love and miss you dearly, Blues Boy Jones, R.I.P.

Back in October 2007, I received a phone call from Opelousas, Louisiana. It was my youngest sister whom I had only seen once. Taneshia Aaron, stated that she had to find her two brothers and sister because she had received a phone call from one of her relatives in Galveston, Texas, concerning our late father's music. Her relatives had some almost unbelievable information about our father's music. Taneshia went on to tell me about our father's old records being sold on E-bay.

What excitement in my heart just hearing from her, and then the good news about our dad's songs being played on the Internet! It was overwhelming and almost hard for me to believe!

For many years I had asked relatives of mine, "What ever happened to our Dad's music?"

To receive great news that his music was being sought over the Internet! Without a doubt, I dedicate this book to my loving sister Taneshia. Sister, I love you dearly. I thank you for making that phone call. It opened doors to start this wonderful journey for me. Also, to let our family, friends and many other people know about our amazing dad, Louis "Blues Boy" Jones and this unforgettable legacy that he left behind.

Dad, I feel you smiling down on us. Words cannot express or tell how much we love and miss you. We thank each person, where ever they are located in this world, from the bottom of our hearts for your loyal and heartfelt support throughout the years. Humbly, we appreciate the love and the respect that you all have shown for Jones' music. Again, I thank each of you kindly and this would not be possible without each of you. Sit back, relax, embrace and enjoy the untold story of the remarkable and talented, legendary Louis "Blues Boy" Jones. After over six decades, Louis "Blues Boy" Jones is still Rockin' the Blues!

Louise Frances Howard Jones

Chapter 1

How Louis met Louise

Of course, there are things in life that young children don't understand. As we grew older my mother did explain to my two brothers and me why our dad was not living in the same household with us. We were very happy children and we loved going to live in Galveston, Texas, with our grandparents during the summertime. It was like living in paradise! As I got a little older, my mother, Louise Frances Howard, told me about one summer in 1952 when her mother, Thyra Anderson, let her spend a few weeks in Galveston, Texas, with her oldest sister Velma Ruth Langston.

Upon approaching Galveston Island, my mother said when she saw all of the water her eyes could not believe it. The beauty and the water seemed endless in her eyesight. She said that it was the most beautiful thing she had ever seen in her life and she would never forget it. She was in awe and excited. She couldn't wait to tell her friends back home in Wharton, Texas, about her grand summer vacation on Galveston Island!

While on vacation, my mother spoke of one night in which her sister Velma, a friend of her sister's named Lillian King, and she went to a dance at the Galveston City Auditorium. My mother said it was so much fun, and she was thrilled with excitement just to be at something as big as this. Living in the city was quite different than back home in Wharton, Texas (a very small rural area).

The guest singer was Ray Charles. My mother could still recall the moment when someone assisted Ray Charles to the stage. She was fourteen years of age and this was something she would never forget! We still talk about that moment in history to this very day. The dance was fun and people were having a real good time.

My mother said all at once she looked around for her sister Velma and she was gone. She was very scared. She started walking around looking for her sister and could not find her. She said she didn't want it to be noticeable how frightened she actually was from being separated from her sister. As she continued to look for Velma and Lillian, she recalled being approached by this young man.

She said this young man said to her, "I know you're looking for your sister and her friend and I can take you to them. They told me to be looking out for you and after the dance they want me to bring you to where they are at."

My mother said she looked at him and told him, "No. I know where my sister is," and she walked off. My mother said she was so afraid; she really didn't know where her sister had gone, but the nerve of some stranger talking about how he could take her to her sister then. Now, my mother was a very beautiful and shapely young lady.

Then my mother said this man went back on stage performing with Ray Charles and his band, but he came to her again and said, "My name is Louis and I don't want hurt you, but your sister and her friend are with some of my friends and they told me to bring you to where they are at."

My mother said to him, "You want hurt me."

He replied, "No, I don't want hurt you." Finally, he did take her to where her sister was and she was so happy to see her big sister. Then my mother said that Louis asked her for her address and she gave it to him. That night a special relationship formed between Louis and Louise.

My mother said that summer in Galveston was an incredible experience. Then meeting a young man who admired her and who was quite charming. For two years, Louis wrote her the most beautiful love letters.

She remembered the mailman, Delbert Tealy, being very excited and he would shout out loudly, "Louise you got mail from Galveston, Texas. A letter from Louis Jones!"

My mother recalled Mr. Tealy being just as happy as she was to hear from Louis Jones. In 1954, when my mother was 16, Louis started performing in Wharton, Texas. He was a traveling musician singing with a band, but always made sure that he would come by and visit with her while in town.

Then the unthinkable happened. My mother said Louis told her she was going to have a baby. My mother said, "No, I am not." My mother was very young, age sixteen at the time, and Louis was twenty-three. With the age difference, she really didn't know much about life, so she did not believe him when he said she was going to be having a baby soon. But as time went on, she knew he was right.

Then the time came when Louis had to travel with his band. They were going to be living in Florida for about four months. Louise said she was afraid because now she had to tell her mom about what had happened and she knew that her mom be upset.

Louis told her that when he returned from Florida, they could get married and that they could have a wedding. My mother said that she was happy and ready to be his wife. My mother was in the eleventh grade, very active in her church and community. She didn't know how her mother would react to the news of her being pregnant. She remembered that her mother became very angry. She said her mother shouted with anger at her because, she felt that Louis being a musician, he was not good for her daughter.

Louise says that her mother told her, "Louis will never marry you Lou; you have just messed up your life." Those were hurtful words.

My mother was very humble and she replied to her mother with a soft voice, "I believe him, Mom. I believe he will marry me just like he said."

Next, my mother recalled receiving mail from Louis in Florida. Enclosed was a money order for her to purchase their marriage license! On March 3, 1955, Louis and Louise were married. She recalled their small, but cute little wedding at her mother's house, located in Spanish Camp (a small rural area near Wharton, Texas). Pastor Alford Hinton Sr. performed the ceremony. My mom recalled all of her sisters crying. She asked them, "Why are you all crying?"

They replied, "Lou, you leaving us."

Then she said to them, "Well, I'm just going to Galveston." My mother recalled that day and time as being one of the happiest moments ever in her life. She said to herself, "I have a husband and now I am ready to start my new life being a wife and soon-to-be mother." The two of them were deeply in love with each other and she said it felt like sitting on top of the world.

Chapter 2

A Dream Come True, with an Unhappy Ending

August 11, 1955, Louis and Louise welcomed Louis Jones III, (our oldest brother) into the world. My mother recalled her husband traveling with his band most of the time. They lived with his mother.

With her being young in age, she often found herself going to church with his mother, Rebecca Prince Jackson. My mother adored her mother-in-law and going to church was something that she was used to doing. She said that it reminded her of being back at home.

My mother recalled her mother-in-law telling her that she should follow her husband sometime. My mother said that this statement hurt her feelings and she felt that Mrs. Jackson no longer wanted her to attend church service with her, or maybe she was getting tired of her and the baby going with her. Perhaps they were getting in the way of something.

My mother soon realized that Mrs. Jackson meant her no harm. She was letting my mother know that as a wife it would be good for a woman to go and see what is going on with her husband, that she did need to spend time with Louis. My mother said she was a little afraid to do this by herself and that she was reluctant about asking her mother-in-law to go with her to see her husband perform.

One day she did ask. My mother went to her mother-in-law and said, "Mrs. Jackson will you go with me to hear Louis sing?"

Mrs. Jackson replied, "Sure I will go with you." My mother said that she was shocked that Mrs. Jackson agreed to go with her to a dance hall. My mother said that when she told her husband that she and his mother would be coming to hear him sing, he explained to her how the ladies acted while he was performing. He went on to tell her how the ladies would be screaming and at times pulling on his clothing.

My mother said to him, "Why do they do that?"

Louis replied, "I really don't know, I guess they really enjoy the music and they like hearing me sing."

And she said, "Okay." One night at a local club in Galveston, Texas, Louis Jones and a band were performing. With her mother-in-law by her side, my mother said sure enough, as Louis was performing the ladies behaved as Louis had described.

The club was packed and she thought to herself, "Boy that cat can sing!" The ladies were screaming! Then she saw some ladies standing near the stage and, yes, they were pulling on her husband. Louis was small in stature and my mother said that she thought, "Those ladies are going to pull my poor husband off the stage." She said that she had to smile because as this was taking place, her husband was looking directly at her and that made her feel good.

Both my mother and her mother-in-law enjoyed hearing Louis sing. They were happy that they attended his performance. My mother said that her husband was a very talented musician and, "Wow, could that man sing!"

Soon, a second son, Harold Leonard Jones, was born on October 8, 1956. My mother said they were still living with his mother Rebecca and not much had changed for Louis and Louise to be able to get their own place. My mother said this was something that she was very unhappy about, no financial support from her husband.

She said that although she didn't lack anything such as food or clothing, she did desire to have their own place. Louis promised her that he would make that happen for her one day. So, Louis continued to travel while leaving Louise home with his mother. Louise was getting tired of this situation because she had no money to go to the stores and buy things that she wanted for herself and her two sons.

Her mother-in-law would spend money on her and the two boys, but my mother said that she felt like that was not how a marriage was supposed to be. She said that she was married to Mrs. Jackson's son and not to her mother-in-law. Louise didn't mind her mother-in-law treating her sometimes, but Rebecca's son needed to be the one providing for his family. My mother said one day she decided to move back home because there had not been any change in the situation of moving into their own place.

Shortly after she was gone, she said Louis came to get her and brought her back to Galveston to his mother's house. This time Louis assured her that it was going to be different and to give him a few months to get things together. Louis promised Louise that as a family they were going to be living in their own home.

September 28, 1957, LaVern Rebecca Jones, their first daughter was born. My mother said nothing else mattered to Louis in this world, "This is my daughter," he said proudly. Life in regards to getting their own place never happened.

My mother said that she was very bitter with our father for not keeping his word. After a third child, my mother told me she went back to Wharton to live and never returned to Galveston. She had to break the cycle of being disappointed over and over again by her husband. It was a hard decision for her to make because she really did love her husband.

She also believed in her heart that she had given him enough time to make a better life for his family. She knew her husband loved her and his children, but his singing career seemed to take priority at the time. Louise said that her three children were her strength and she had to make a life for us. It was a struggle, but my mother got us a place to stay. She did the best that she could do raising us with no father in the home.

Life at times seemed so unfair and all we had to hold onto was our faith in a higher power. While writing this book in November 2013, my thoughts about life were these: God we give thanks to you for bringing us out of the storms that clouded our minds, our visions and our daily existence.

Chapter 3

Who Was Louis Jones?

Let's travel back in time to when I was a teenager. I would like to share with the world my thoughts and experiences on the topic: who is Louis Jones?

My two brothers and I had been spending our summers in Galveston, Texas, since we were young children. Each summer, a relative would travel from Galveston to pick us up or my mother Louise would get someone to take us to stay with our Grandmother, Rebecca Prince Jackson, in Galveston.

My grandmother's house was located at 909, 37th Street on the corner of Broadway. What fond memories of beautiful Galveston Island I have. As we spent time with family and friends, it was truly unforgettable.

Every time my grandmother said to us, "Your dad will come by and see you all on tomorrow," my heart started to race with excitement. I was not going to rest well the night before. I could not wait until my eyes looked upon my dad's face and I loved to hear my dad speak. Although he was talking, his words seemed like music in my ears.

I would look at him and wonder, "What is it about my dad that seems different?" I was just puzzled about him. I had never really asked him about his life. My mother told us that our father recorded his first song titled, "Rock n Roll Bells," in 1956 on the Peacock Record label under Don Robey, located in Houston, Texas.

As a young child, I remember my uncle Andrew Prince Johnson Sr., giving us one of my dad's records to play on a blue and white phonograph. Uncle Andrew was my dad's oldest brother. My grandmother's youngest sister, Emily Prince Robinson, whom we called Aunt Nuna, would come down from Houston to visit her. I remember these visits were usually on a Friday.   This would happen each time my Aunt Nuna would see my dad because he was going to bring fish for them to fry on that Friday or the next day, Saturday.

As soon as my dad entered the house, my Aunt Nuna would shout with so much joy and excitement in her voice, "Jones, look at my nephew, a blues singer, he traveled the world and made records, aww Jones you something else!"

I would be sitting on the sofa listening to all of this, as a young teenager and I was wondering in my mind, "What is my Aunt Nuna talking about? She's saying that my Dad traveled the world and made records, Wow!"

What made me realize that there was something very special about my dad was the way he would react each time Aunt Nuna greeted him like that. All my dad would do, with a slight smile on his face, was just say, "Hey Aunt Nuna."

My thoughts to this day are how humble a man my dad was. He never said anything more than those few words. One summer back in the early seventies, my dad dropped by and wanted my two brothers and me to come over to his apartment so we could spend some time together with him. At that time he was dating a lady by the name of Mrs. Esther Ruth. They lived in the Parkland Apartments.

While walking over to the apartments which were just around the corner, my dad started telling us that he knew Della Reese. He said that she was his friend and that she autographed her picture for him. Then he went on to say that he knew singers B. B. King and Ray Charles. He received a chance to perform with them on stage in his early days in the music business.

My dad exclaimed that he met boxer Cassius Clay. He told us that in 1963, he traveled to New York City and recorded a song called, "The Birds Is Coming," on the Decca Record Label. He said the song was released around the same time as the Alfred Hitchcock movie called *The Birds* was in theaters.

He went on to say that one time he and his band members lived in Bermuda for about six months playing at a local club there. He said, "Bermuda, you know that's out of the United States?"

I replied with excitement, "Really Dad!" My thoughts were, "These are famous people that you see on TV or hear over the radio. Wow! My Dad knows these people, Wow! This is something big."

While at the apartment, my two brothers and I were listening to a radio in the living room. Our dad had gone into another room.

When he came to where we were, he said, "You all listening to that music?"

And we replied, "Yes, Daddy."

Then dad said, "Aw. That ain't no music. Have you all ever heard me sing?"

We replied, "No, daddy."

Then my dad started singing to us. I was mesmerized by his voice back then and still am today. I do not know anyone that I can compare his voice to. Truly the voice of an angel. I was like, "This is our dad and he can sing like that!" I was in a trance. Oh! What a voice. Wow! My mother was right when she made the statement back then and I totally agreed with her. That man can sing and that man is my dad!

Chapter 4

Time Brings about Change

LaVern Rebecca Jones, age 19.

During my senior year in high school, back in 1975, my mother gave me permission to live with my grandmother, Rebecca P. Jackson. This was something that I looked forward to and I knew this was going to be a privilege to live on Galveston Island. Most important was just being with my grandmother whom I loved so much. I would be able to see my dad more.

Before I graduated, I remember my dad and his new wife Patricia giving me a Polaroid camera and a brown suede coat with fur around the neck. It was a beautiful coat. I will forever love Galveston Island. The love I have in my heart for my family is unmeasurable.

After graduating from Ball High School in Galveston in May, 1976, I decided to move back home with my mother in Wharton, Texas and I started a new job. It wasn't very long after that, I met my first husband Roy Lee Jackson Sr.

When I had my first daughter LaRoysha Marlette Jackson, on September 16, 1977, I couldn't wait to take my beautiful baby girl to meet her grandparents and great-grandparents in Galveston. I was so excited. My dad was so happy and proud of his granddaughter. He held her and I took pictures of them with the camera he had given me for graduation. It was such a precious moment.

Then on October 3, 1981, we celebrated the arrival of my second daughter Roylisha Monique Jackson. Being married and taking care of my children brought about a change in my life because we didn't get to visit my relatives who lived in Galveston, Texas as much as we used to.

Sometimes, I believe people wish that they could go back in time and relive some of the choices that they had made. In life there are certain wrong choices that we make. I believe that if somehow a person was given the opportunity to redo something, a person would definitely do things in a totally different way. No one enjoys pain or suffering. In reality it will never be done, so we are to live our lives to the fullest and make the right choices to have very few regrets later in life, if possible.

Chapter 5

Changes, Devastating

Life was good and from time to time my husband Roy Lee, would take us to visit my family on Galveston Island. This was always such a special time for me and very dear to my heart. I just loved being around family and friends. I have always felt that nothing in this world can take the place of our loved ones.

In January 1982, my grandmother Rebecca called me and said that she had been sick with a cold. She teased me about not coming to see her and I remember her saying, "Levern, (that's what she called me) don't love your grandmother anymore?"

I said, "Of course, Grama, (that's what we called her) you know I love you." We were both laughing away; she understood about the children, but she went on to tell me not to let so much time go by without coming to see about her.

On March 12, 1982, I received a phone call that devastated our family. My grandmother Rebecca had died. She was at home. Life would never be the same. Immediately, I thought about my dad because his mother was his world; he never knew his father.

My grandmother Rebecca often told us how she spoiled my dad. He was the baby of his siblings. The family knew that if my dad had any problems, he could always go to his mother's house. I remember when I was a very young girl, my grandmother told me that if her son needed a place to lay his head down or if he needed food to eat, her door would always be open. I know for a fact that there is nothing like a mother's love for her child or children.

I don't understand to this day why I let so much time go by without going back to Galveston. I still kept in contact with my dad's only sister, Laura Mae O'Neal. We wrote letters to each other. Also, at times I did talk on the telephone with his oldest brother, my Uncle Andrew. I would just ask my Aunt Laura if she had seen my dad and she said that she had not seen him. I remember leaving a shirt with my Aunt Laura to give to my dad for Father's Day. Losing their mother shattered the family.

My dad was closer to his mother than to his siblings. My dad loved singing blues music back in the early 1950s and 60s. My aunt and uncle had their careers, but they thought that their brother should have done something different with his life because in the end, his music career didn't bring him much success.

I often thought about my dad because I felt that he was hurting and yet it was still hard for me knowing that my grandmother was gone. In April 1983, I received a terrifying telephone call from my stepmother Pat. She told me that my dad had suffered a stroke and he was admitted to John Sealy Hospital in Galveston, Texas. Pat told me that my dad was doing all right and I told her that I would come to the hospital and see him as fast as we could get there.

Quickly, my husband and I went to the hospital. While there, my dad was talking. He said that he was going to be all right and for me not to worry. I felt good about the situation, but I was a little worried because I didn't know much about what a stroke was. We said good-bye and we looked forward to visiting my dad in Galveston to catch up on some lost time or at least try and then talk about the good ole days.

A few days later Pat called again. This time she had more news about my father's health and it was not good. I was torn apart when Pat told me that my dad had suffered several strokes and that he was in a coma. Pat went on to tell me that she and my father were not getting along well in their marriage and that she wanted him to leave. When he lost his mother, Pat said that they tried to mend their marriage but they had another terrible argument and he fell with a stroke in their home.

Pat told me that my dad had bad headaches for about eight years, but he chose not to see a doctor. I can't explain why I never went to see my father when he was in a nursing home for over a year. By this time my mother and my siblings were all living in San Francisco, California.

My marriage was not stable either. But November 3, 1983, I gave birth to my third child. My son, Leelan Rashad Prince Jackson! After having two adorable girls, my son was my pride and joy. Children bring heavenly joy into your life. Yet, going through a divorce can be the ugliest experience in life anyone will ever have to face.

Early June 1984, I received a phone call from my Uncle Andrew. He told me that my dad was in a nursing home in Clute, Texas. We were living in Old Ocean, Texas and these two locations were just a few miles apart. I was happy about seeing my father, but in my heart I knew that seeing him in this condition was going to make me very sad because in reality no one wants to see a love one hurting or suffering.

I had to explain to my daughters in the best way I could about their grandfather and seeing him. They were young but I knew that they were going to be all right and my son was only a few months old. My husband took us to see my dad at the Woodlake Nursing Home located on Plantation Street in Clute, Texas.

When I saw my dad for the first time since he had lost his mother, it was hard for me to hold back my tears. I was use to seeing him so vibrant and full of life. His facial features looked good and he did have some movement. I leaned close to talk to him and tell him that his grandchildren were there to see him. I introduced the kids to him and he did move his eyes.

I told my dad that the kids and I were getting ready to go on a trip to visit family out in San Francisco and when we got back from our trip, we would come by and check on him. With teary eyes I kissed my dad's face and told him, "I love you."

My heart ached to leave him. As I was preparing for the trip, my mind was on my father. I was concerned about his health but I was also excited about seeing my family in California. In life we just want the best for our families and friends, but when someone is ill, I am a firm believer in prayer. So I continued to pray for a change in my dad's condition and for all people to better themselves.

We were on our way to California, traveling by bus. It was just me and my children, but I forgot to give my dad his Father's Day card. I was upset about that. Immediately, I called my husband and told him to please take my dad his Father's Day card.

"Please, read it to him out loud for me, then place the card on the nightstand by his bed," I said.

California was grand as ever. We dined at some of the best restaurants and we saw some of the most breathtaking and beautiful scenic views in the world! Beyond everything in life to me, it was important to know that my family was doing well. That meant the most to me above all things.

It was time to leave The Bay Area of San Francisco. Our good-byes were tearful but, we were extremely happy for the time that we spent together with one another. Again, the love for family is unmeasurable. My husband was there to pick us up from the bus station only to greet me with devastating news.

I screamed out loud, "Oh God! Oh God! My dad is dead." I was crushed. Never had I felt so much pain within my heart and down to my very soul. I thought it was the beginning, yet it was the end. I thought that when I returned home from the trip that my family and I would be spending a great amount of time with my father at the nursing home. It was as if time stood still and my father was gone.

We got back from the trip on a Friday and the funeral was the very next day, Saturday. One could only imagine how tired I was. At his service, I was totally out of it. I could not even think straight and at times I don't remember what was going on. I felt as though I was in a state of shock.

I didn't go to his burial; I couldn't. At home, it was a daily struggle for me as I tried to pull myself together after the loss of my dad, realizing it wasn't going to be easy. Pat told me in another conversation we had, that my dad said after losing his mother he had nothing to live for. My heart ached even more. With tears in my eyes, I told Pat that he had us; he had his children and grandchildren to live for.

This statement that my father made hurt me deeply for years and years and I will never understand it as long as I live. At times, I still cry today... Again, this is very emotional...

Chapter 6

Still Searching for Answers

Year after year, I continued to search for the answers to whatever happened to our dad's music. I received the same feedback as before from my mother and uncle. By this time, I was divorced and making sure that I provided for my children's well-being, but I would not stop searching for answers to my dad's music. In my heart I felt that there was something big out there, but I had not found the right people who could help me with my search.

My mother said that she was under the age of eighteen when she married my father and she didn't get to travel often with our father while he performed. She stated she knew very little about the business side of his career. Also, my mother said that he really didn't discuss much with her about his music.

Before Louis met Louise, my Uncle Andrew stated that he and my dad were very young men, and while living in Houston, Texas his brother Louis came to live with him. My uncle stated his brother entered a talent show that was held every Saturday. My uncle said for months that his brother would come in first place every time, won a trophy, and was featured in the newspaper.

I realized that my father was extremely talented way back then and music seemed to be his greatest passion early in his life. My Uncle Andrew told me for the second time about "Rock n Roll Bells". This song was on the Peacock record label, producer/owner Don Robey, located in Houston, Texas, circa 1956. Uncle Andrew said that his brother went into the studio one day (he said that the studio seemed as if it was his brother's second home), to record a song and Don Robey gave my father cash money for his work, strictly for his first recording which was "Rock n Roll Bells".

My uncle said that back then when he would mention to his brother that he believed that for my dad's best interest, it would be wise for him to hire an attorney to protect his rights as a recording music artist. My Uncle Andrew often told me how my father wouldn't listen to him and that his brother just continued to do things his own way, yet my uncle felt that with an attorney, his brother would have had some type of protection for his music later in his life.

Also, my uncle told me that his brother did back-up singing for many of the blues and gospel artists on the Peacock record label. My uncle would tell me about the many times that singer B. B. King would call their mother's home looking for Louis to go on tour with him, but the two never connected as far as touring together because my dad would be on tour for himself.

I was intrigued by all of this. The news that someone was using an instrumental version of the song "Rock n Roll Bells" for a TV commercial ad for a car dealership located in Houston, Texas, brought great joy to my heart. This was told to me by my Uncle Andrew, yet he said that he only heard the song a few times and he believed someone removed it for legal purposes. My uncle told me that he knew that his brother had recorded about four or five records and my mother only recalled one records.

This picture was taken in the early 1950s, somewhere in the Houston, Texas area. Jones is at the mic.

Blues Boy Jones at the mic doing
what he loved the best...singing the
blues! (The location unknown). I do not
know the musicians in these photos.

Remember, we still didn't know who had control over Jones' music. A period of about twenty-three years has passed and much had changed in my life but, my dad was on my mind often throughout those years. I missed seeing him dearly and hearing his unique voice. In October 2011, I received a phone call that turned things upside down regarding Blues Boy Jones' music. The call came from Taneshia Aaron, my younger half-sister that I had only met once before. I recalled when my father had dated a lady named Marie Aaron years ago in Galveston. Taneshia resided in Opelousas, Louisiana at that time.

She called me with information that we needed to know concerning our late father's music. She stated that some of her family members who lived in Galveston, Texas, informed her that our late father's music was being sold on E-Bay. Taneshia said that she had to find her siblings and inform us about this because we needed to come together and find out who had the rights to our father's music. We are his legal heirs, his four children. It had been a long time coming and just hearing from my sister meant the world to me.

With my sister having news about our dad's music on such a large scale such as this, I was screaming, shouting and crying tears of joy. Who would have ever thought that twenty-three years later, Louis (Blues Boy) Jones' music would be on the Internet? I was at a loss for words. This was a joyful time in my life and I felt that it was the beginning of something grand for our dad's music, somewhat of a miracle.

Taneshia had only seen our dad a few times in her life. She was very young when he passed away and she did not attend his service. Of course, we tried to catch up on things as we talked about old times and the present time. There were a lot of things she wanted to know about our father.

Taneshia said that her family had moved away and lived in Chicago, Illinois for a long period of time, and then they returned to their hometown which was Opelousas, Louisiana. We enjoyed our conversations and then it was time for us to go to work to see, if at all possible, what we could find out about our dad's music. The main thing we were concerned about was the rights to his music.

Immediately, I went to the library to see what information I could find, because I did not have a computer in my home. Then I recalled asking a longtime friend of mine, Jen Ross Johnson, to look up information about my dad's music.

Jen told me that a song titled: "Come on Home" was being sold on various CDs statewide. This totally blew my mind! I could not believe what I was hearing. My dad's music, after all these years, was on the Internet. Wow!

At the library, I researched literature on Don Robey and read the story about him as founder of Peacock Records, which was located in Houston, Texas. Then I saw "Rock n Roll Bells" in the Peacock archives. Amazing! Things were starting to unfold about the history of Jones' music. It was a long wait and worth every second. I saw another song titled: "Someway, Somewhere".

I had the biggest smile on my face discovering all of this about our dad's music. I felt very proud of him as an artist. This was beyond my wildest dreams, but I eagerly awaited the journey that lay ahead! This was good news, but I believed something on an even grander scale was right around the corner for Louis (Blues Boy) Jones' music!

My family was very excited for us. We have discovered something about his music and we live in a different era. With access to the Internet, information was more available. One night while visiting my oldest daughter and her family in Clute, Texas, Taneshia, my daughter, and I were on a three-way telephone conversation while looking onto computers in each of our homes. We somehow were able to access and listen to "Come on Home". It was one of the happiest moments in our lives, no doubt history in the making. Just hearing my dad's voice again gave life a new meaning to me.

After all these years of searching for answers, whoever would have thought that this would be made possible? Truly this was a miracle from God. I was thrilled because LaRoysha was one of my dad's older grand-daughters and this was her grandfather with songs on the Internet, just a priceless moment and one to cherish for a lifetime. Again, I cried happy and joyful tears, almost unbelievable!

I searched the Internet periodically and I was happy, but deep down within, I knew eventually more information would appear about my dad's music. He had such a beautiful voice and he could really sing. His voice was very gifted and one of a kind to me.

Chapter 7

Really Good News!

It was hard to believe that four years had passed. On May 27, 2011, I was about to leave for work one evening and when I received a strange phone call from someone named Jeremy Pender, who had an accent. He said that he was calling me from the United Kingdom. Jeremy explained to me who he was, why he was calling and that he was responding after reading a blog site over the Internet that Louis (Blues Boy) Jones' children were seeking advice about their father's music.

This request was sent by Jones' youngest daughter Taneshia Aaron, back in January 2011. Jeremy spoke with Taneshia first and he told me that Taneshia had given him my phone number. She stated that he should give me a call because I would have more information pertaining to our dad than she did. My dear sister sure knows how to reach out and get in touch with people. I am so grateful for her boldness. This opened up new doors about Jones' music and we came across some really good news.

Jeremy Pender went on to explain to me that he was an investigator and helped people try to locate family members and friends, or if people were seeking legal advice about anyone who may need advice involving any type of unresolved business matters. I shared stories about my dad's amazing life with Jeremy. He knew a lot of things about my father's music, yet he still didn't know who had control over the copyrights.

More important, Jeremy stated that if we could find the right people to help us locate Jones' master tapes; that would help greatly. He explained that the master tapes are stored somewhere in a company's archives. Also, he told me to understand that this might take some time and that it would not be something done overnight. I understood, but I was willing and ready for the ride. I wanted to give honor and respect to my dad's legacy.

We hope to have a CD reissued of his music, as we, his children, are his legal heirs. We want to claim ownership over our father's music if at all possible. Jeremy said that he would try to contact all parties involved in the Blues Boy Jones' music era. He said that when he contacted some of the relatives that had family members who once sang or played instruments on those old records, that some of the people showed very little interest and this was puzzling to him.

Oh! What a joy for me as history unfolded. This was my dad and I wanted to honor him and his music in any way that I possibly could. Picture this, it was twenty-seven years later and Louis (Blues Boy) Jones', music from the 1950s and 1960s was being recognized on this level, the Internet, and then receiving a phone call from a man from the United Kingdom about his music was priceless! I told Jeremy that as long as I lived, this would be one of the most unforgettable moments in my life. I thanked him over and over again for calling me and giving me some of the greatest news ever about my dad's music and for initially making contact with my sister.

My thoughts were: what an act of kindness. The fact that Jeremy cared meant the most to me. Jeremy went on to tell me about Joe Smith. He said that Joe Smith played in a band called The Bobby Scott Orchestra, of which my father was the lead singer, on the records titled: "Come on Home" and "I'll Be your Fool". Jeremy also informed me that Joe would be calling me. The excitement of this was beyond my wildest dream.

I believed that I was above cloud 9! I shared this good news with family and friends. They were so happy for me because they knew that it had been a struggle for me. I had been searching for many years trying to find information and the location of my father's music. Finally, for me it was good to hear great news!

Although Jeremy called me from time to time, he told me to get a computer in my home because with a computer there, I would be able to access information worldwide. I was in my early 50s at that time and I knew very little about computers, but in reality it was time for a change.

In June 2011, somehow Joe Smith and I missed phone calls from one another. Then we finally connected. We were happy to stop playing phone tag as we laughed. Joe went on to tell me how he missed his old friend, and I cried. We agreed that this was a big moment in history for both of us. The music that he and my dad shared — what precious memories for both of us.

I thought it was marvelous that after all these years, I received an opportunity to talk with one of my dad's friends. The feeling was unexplainable. Joe said that he was in just as much disbelief, talking to his friend Louis' daughter after all these years. My thoughts were what an amazing God! I cried some, again tears of joy.

Joe and I laughed as we walked down memory lane about my dad's life and the many wonderful things that the two of them had shared when my father was living. This really touched my heart when Joe said that my father was so very talented and that he really should have made it big in the music industry like some of the other great entertainers in that era, such as Ray Charles, B. B. King, Bobby Blue Bland and others.

Joe said that what my Dad had lacked was a good manager. I felt heartbroken for my dad. Some of my family members felt the same way and that my dad had mentioned to some of them that he wasn't treated fairly during his music career.

I thought to myself: what is it that I can do to honor my dad's music and his legacy? We wanted some type of validation for his music. I felt that he was deserving of that. Many people have told me that my father was an extremely talented musician; he was a great entertainer and even considered one of the best. Joe told me about the time when the band traveled overseas to Bermuda. They stayed there for about six months and performed at this club called The Play House Inn.

Joe said they had a blast! He laughed as he thought about how all of the band members were dating one of those island girls. Joe said that he was getting excited just thinking back about how those beautiful island girls would be talking to them with an accent. Joe and I both were laughing. I truly enjoyed our conversations, and Joe said he was so happy to be talking with me about that time in their lives so long ago. Joe said that he knew that my father would be very proud me. I felt very privileged for being given such a remarkable opportunity as this.

Joe said that as very young men, he and my father recorded their first song together at a studio in Beaumont, Texas. He remembered that he wanted to lead that song, but the man who owned the studio liked my father's voice and wanted him to lead instead. Joe said that Lelan Rogers, the brother of country singer Kenny Rogers, was the producer of Sabra Records then located in Houston, Texas. The song called "I'll Be Your Fool" was written by my father and the flipside of the record was "Someway Somewhere".

Then Joe went on to tell me about the time that they performed at this club in LaMarque, Texas called G and M Pleasure Spot. Joe said that a lot of big entertainers were featured there such as Ike and Tina Turner, B. B. King, Little Milton, and many others. On this particular night, Joe said that after my father and the band finished performing at G and M Pleasure Spot, this lady by the name of Maxine Brown approached them with a proposition.

Joe said they found out Maxine Brown was a known recording artist. Maxine was accompanied by her hair hairstylist and a personal traveling friend and songwriter, Verdell Mack. Maxine told them that when she heard their performance, she was very impressed with their talent. Maxine told them the she liked their style and that one day she would send for them to visit her in New York City to go on tour.

Joe said that they were very excited about an offer to travel to New York City. Also they were very eager and ready for such an adventure. When they finally received the invitation from Maxine, she told them that she would be sending one of her personal drivers to pick them up.

In 1962, when the driver arrived in Galveston, Joe said that they had packed a lot of luggage. They were very young men and you could only imagine all of the excitement. They loaded the car up and were on their way, but the driver soon realized that the car was moving very slowly and it was hard for him to drive.

Then the driver said, "We are not going to make it to New York City. You all have too much shit." Joe and I laughed.

The driver said to them, "Have you all ever traveled before? You all will have to get rid of some of your things at the next bus stop."

"Everyone will have to ship some of your things back home," he continued. So they did. Joe said that they really didn't know to travel lightly and that they didn't want to run out of anything. Joe said that the memories of him and all of his friends having so much fun as they traveled the world were unforgettable. They had the time of their lives.

Before reaching New York, Joe said they stopped in several states: Oklahoma, Illinois, West Virginia, and others. Joe said that because of time and his health, he needed more time to remember some of the things that they experienced. I told Joe many people will never experience anything on that level, although some will, but I am most proud that my dad and the rest of the band members did make a difference while in the music industry. They all left a great mark in the history of music!

Joe said that he didn't understand why he was the last one living of Louis (Blues Boy) Jones and the Bobby Scott Orchestra Band but, he was thankful to God. During our conversation, Joe did inform me about the passing of another great friend. In January 2010, Patrick Williams, the dynamic trumpet player for the band, passed away. Patrick was from Galveston, Texas and Joe said that he did attend the service.

Joe and I still call each another from time to time. I let Mr. Smith know that I was very grateful for that moment in time when our paths crossed. It was a pleasure talking with someone who knew my dad—first, as a good friend and then for the fact that he still admired my dad's talents. Joe shared with me that he went on to play guitar for thirteen years with the world known group The Four Tops, under music producer Berry Gordy of Motown Records. That was more great news, absolutely amazing!

I have come to the conclusion that people will share many life stories with each other or perhaps in a group, but in reality you just can't tell it all; it is impossible.

Chapter 8

Worldwide Recognition

In August 2011, I decided to track my dad's songs that were viewed on the Internet, mainly on YouTube. I did this on a daily basis or whenever possible. These songs were uploaded by people in places around the world! One day it hit me and I thought to myself: what is it that I could do to let the people know how much I truly appreciate them sharing my father's music?

I noticed that my sister Taneshia had made a comment on one of our dad's songs. The comment was directed to a follower of his music and that person replied with such a beautiful and kind comment. It was special to us and very touching. I was in my mid-fifties at the time and was a little reluctant about computers, but I knew in life that you have to take a chance sometimes or like one might say, get out of your comfort zone.

I logged onto the names of the people that had made comments about Jones' music. I was completely in awe! People in places from all around the world loved and respected my dad's music; I couldn't believe it. I was overwhelmed with joy and I thought in my mind that I could never pay anyone for a moment such as this. It was simply priceless. I would forever cherish all these moments as long as I live and I was so grateful to each and every follower of my dad's music!

I sent a thank you note to several followers of my dad's music. Three of them replied back and I cried tears of happiness. Never in my life did I know that people cared, respected, or had so much love for Blues Boy Jones' music. I thank God. It is a beautiful thing in life when an entertainer's music can touch people in places worldwide. This almost left me speechless. Again what an honor and also an act of universal love for my dad's legacy. Dad you are still so amazing!

The three people who replied to me personally by e-mail had the kindest words about my dad's music. They were: The Monobaby from The United Kingdom, Glendoras from Sweden, and Moniculups from Italy. Truly I was grateful!

Next, I came up with another idea that I needed to let family and friends know about all of this. So I decided I would write a newspaper article and then one day, I would have a book published about my dad's life. Sometimes as I browsed the Internet, I discovered that people had an interest and they asked questions among themselves such as: "What did Jones look like? Where was he from? Does anyone have pictures of him? Are there any more records of his besides, 'Come on Home?' Please let me know."

I started making phone calls or I left messages with different newspaper companies in Galveston County and other local newspaper companies in the area. An editor by the name of Michael Durisseau responded and I told him about my late father's accomplishments.

Michael said, yes, right away that he wanted to print such a loving story and that my story was very special and people did need to read about this. I cried and I couldn't thank him enough. What excitement and joy! An article titled, "Jazz legend's music seeing revival", made the front page of *The Post* newspaper on September 7, 2011! This was history made for Jones and his family again. Twenty-seven years later, Jones was making news about his music. I was at a loss for words!

Could this really be happening? I was beyond grateful and I felt like I was on top of the world! Dad, I thank you for leaving such beautiful yet timeless music for people to enjoy in different locations all around the globe. The many dedicated followers of my father's music in areas across the globe throughout these years was the reason that his legacy still lived on. For that, I humbly thank each of you from the bottom of my heart!

Still I wanted more recognition for my dad's music. I called up the *Brazoria County News*, the *Wharton Journal-Spectator* and *Forward Times* to see if they would feature an article about the life of blues singer Louis (Blues Boy) Jones. Jeremy Pender and Joe Smith have kept in touch. Jeremy has been e-mailing record companies galore to find information on Jones' music and told me that he wanted me to join Facebook. He insisted that I could reach out to more people through this website.

Facebook seemed like fun and I did get a chance to communicate with family and friends almost daily. Also, it was a joy making new friends. Early in June 2012, Mickey Nold requested my friendship on Facebook through Jeremy Pender and I did accept Mickey's request. Mickey told Jeremy that he admired me for what I was doing for my father's music. How kind and very thoughtful of Mickey. It meant a lot to me just for him to acknowledge my efforts. Mickey sent me a message that he wanted to dedicate a song to me. I felt very fortunate and I greatly appreciated him. Big shout out to Mickey!

Mickey is a radio DJ. He told us the date and time that this dedication was going to take place and I was prepared. Then I realized that I missed the program. I was terribly disappointed in myself that I had missed the show because I forgot about the difference in our time zones. When I e-mailed Jeremy he said that he was also sorry that I had missed the show.

Then I looked at my Facebook page and Mickey sent a message to us that if we missed the show, just log onto this blog site and that the dedication to Louis (Blues Boy) Jones' daughter LaVern was in the archives. Talk about one very happy and blessed lady! How ironic was that?

It was almost Father's Day in June 1984 when my dad passed away, and it was twenty-eight years later the dedication took place on Saturday, June 16, 2012. Father's day was that Sunday. What a thrill of a lifetime. I could have fainted when I heard Mickey Nold speak with that English accent that I love to hear. Mickey said, "Jeremy Pender told me about blues singer Louis Blues Boy Jones. He was quite an entertainer in the 1950s and 1960s. I requested his daughter's friendship on Facebook. She is LaVern Jones Lemons from Wharton, Texas. I want to dedicate one her father's songs to her. Here it is, 'Someway Somewhere.' and I hope she likes it."

It was one of the best gifts ever in my life and I would cherish this priceless moment to infinity. Mickey Nold lives in Birmingham, United Kingdom, and this dedication was over live radio all the way from the United Kingdom just for lil' ole me. Again, priceless! Thanks a million Mickey. You were the best!

I had to share this about when I was a young teenager in the early seventies. I loved music and almost every night I couldn't wait to turn my radio on and listen to this radio station starting at 10:00 p.m. I would listen to this radio station until I would fall asleep. It was called "Randy at Night" and this radio station was located in Nashville, Tennessee. Every now and then I would hear this particular song and my thoughts were, *Wow! I sure do like that song and the beat of it.*

Then I thought whoever was singing that song sure could sing. One day my Uncle Andrew and I were talking and I happened to mention to him about how I used to love listening to that radio station out of Nashville, Tennessee at night.

My uncle said, "Oh! Yeah, Randy at Night'". Then he said, "They played your father's records and I use to hear them." And then it hit me, the record that I heard and loved so much was "Someway, Somewhere" and at that time I didn't know that it was my very own father.

I still became so emotional just thinking about all those wonderful things that my dad did in his lifetime. My dad was such an amazing man. I am so thankful and blessed to be able to share all of these beautiful stories and his legacy with everyone. My father touched so many lives, in so many ways, again just unforgettable memories.

In December 2011, Jones had about 2,000 views on YouTube. These were the songs that people could log on and listen to: "Rock n Roll Bells" on Peacock Record Label; "Come on Home", "I'll Be Your Fool", "Someway, Somewhere", on Sabra Records; and "That's Cuz I Love You" and "The Birds is Coming", on Decca Records.

I continued every now and then to make phone calls to the newspaper companies that I mentioned earlier, still hoping that someone would print another article on my father. On April 4, 2013, an article titled "Jones' legacy gains popularity" was featured in *The Brazoria County News*. It was a great article and the editor did a fantastic job. I thanked her dearly.

Jeremy Pender often said that whenever he came to visit his friends in the United States, he wanted to meet Blues Boy Jones' daughter and her family. Jeremy was the kindest man that I knew and I felt like he was my friend for a lifetime. He was so incredible and he really had a big heart. He was very caring. I know that some things just don't come with a price. Jeremy called me a few months prior and told me that he would be traveling to the United States with a friend, Maria.

On April 13, 2013, we were anticipating meeting for the first time. Over the top excited! A longtime friend of mine, Jen Ross Johnson, Alan Johnson, and I made plans to go down to Galveston, Texas. I wanted to show Jeremy where my dad's mother once lived. Also, this was the place where my two brothers and I had spent our summers. We wanted to make sure that we visited this place called Selena Blue Room. Selena was in business for over fifty years. This club in the early days was where all the musicians (some famous) hung out. My uncle and stepmother told me that Selena was well known in the music industry.

Saturday, April 13, 2013, the five of us (Jeremy, Maria, Jen, Alan) and myself had the most fabulous time on Galveston Island. We took pictures at 909 37th Street.

All the way from Market Weighton, United Kingdom, my dear friends Jeremy Pender and his friend Maria Garza Schumacher.

No one was living at the address when this picture was taken.

The front porch at 909 37th Broadway Street, the address in which my late grandmother Rebecca (Jones' mother) resided for many years. The house was occupied in this photo.

We shared many stories, ate good seafood and looked at a lot of historical sights. We just had a great time together. We took pictures at the famous Selena's Blue Room as well. While at Selena's place, as it was no longer open, we saw some men next to the place. We asked them if they could give us some history about Selena's or if they knew anyone who would. The men were very helpful and told us about Mr. Leon Banks Jr. They said that Mr. Banks was a longtime friend of Selena's.

We told the men that we wanted to meet Mr. Banks so they called him up and Mr. Banks said, "Sure."

We informed the men that I was the late Louis Jones' daughter and I wanted to meet and talk to people who remembered my father. As we approached Mr. Banks' home and as we were getting out of our cars, we did notice an older man sitting in a chair. It appeared to me that he was holding an object in his hand. Also, I noticed that his eyesight wasn't the best; one eye was slightly closed. We carefully approached him and we announced who we were and he greeted us.

But I laughed to myself because I realized that Mr. Banks didn't trust us. When I told him who I was and that I was Louis Jones' oldest daughter, Mr. Banks seemed to come to life. He brought tears to my eyes when he told us that he didn't want us to leave and that it had been a very long time since he had this much fun. We brightened up his world that day talking about the good old days. I gave him newspaper articles and pictures of my dad and he said that he would forever cherish them.

We laughed when he said this, "Your daddy could sing, but he was a mama's boy." That was a true statement. My uncle often told me that when my father was on tour, he would constantly call their mother and that he would get homesick. Also, there had been times that my father left the band and returned home.

Before we left, Mr. Banks put away the screwdriver he was holding and we understood. He was eighty-five years old and we were strangers at first but, before we left, we became friends. Mr. Banks and I continued to talk on the phone, wrote letters to each other, and visited when possible. He had so much history and he was just an awesome friend. He told me that my father was a great man and that I should be proud of him.

I told Mr. Banks, "Thank you and I am very proud to be his daughter." I let Mr. Banks know that I was grateful that our paths crossed. Mr. Leon Banks Jr., my dear friend, was then 86 years old. Also, he told me that he truly missed his lifetime friend, the late Selena Fulton. She owned and operated her business (Selena Blue Room) for about fifty years.

Mr. Leon my dear friend for life, that was what he told me often. He was quite a gentleman!

Sunday April 14, 2013, Jeremy and Maria told us that they felt like royalty because they got to meet my two daughters and my five grandchildren. My oldest daughter LaRoysha was a great cook. She had prepared a four course meal with dessert at Jen's house. It was fabulous and delicious. Jeremy was so delighted to have met some of Blues Boy Jones' grandchildren and great grandchildren. At times even words are not enough to express all the joyous things that you experience in life.

On YouTube, Jones' views were climbing higher everyday as people around the world listened to his music. At one point, there were about five songs on the Internet and now there are nine songs. These songs are uploaded and viewed from his followers in places all over the world. Some of the locations are: The United Kingdom, Sweden, Italy, France, Germany, Japan, Trinidad & Tobago, Austria, Australia, Canada, Africa, Greece, Aruba, Spain, Switzerland, Belgium, the United States of America, and recently the Galapagos Island. I am sure there are more places around the globe!

Many of Jones' followers have
made the kindest and most heartfelt
comments about his music. Some of the
comments are written in other
languages. What an honor that my dad's
music was capable of bringing people of
all nationalities together. It was too
amazing. Someone made a comment
that Jones came on the music scene in
the early 1960s, but once he switched
from singing blues to soul music, he fell
through the cracks and was never heard
of again.

That statement truly made my heart sad. Many people still couldn't put a face to any of my father's music, so I decided to purchase one of his records, "Come on Home." My dad wrote this song and it seems to be this most popular. I was truly excited to be holding one of my dad's records, history and priceless! I have a cousin who was a very talented musician and songwriter. His name was Phil O'Neal, but we called him Mookie. I told Mookie to help me upload a song called "I Cried" that was written by my dad and was on the flipside of "Come on Home". "I Cried": I love this song and the instruments were mind-blowing!

When I made that comment, a man by the name of Ronnie Rocket sent a comment to me from Berlin, Germany! Ronnie went on to say that he loved all of the wonderful things that I said about my father and that he was going to send any information that I wrote about my father to social networks. Now, I was feeling blessed all over again! I sent much appreciation and thanks to Ronnie Rocket a billion times. He was the coolest guy that I knew in Berlin, Germany!

Ronnie had a blog site called News Music United. There have been times that a few of Jones' songs made News Music United Top 20 Chart on this blog site. I realized that those songs were the oldest, as far as the year made, and yet Jones music was still making the charts and making history. Wow! There was also an All Time Top 100 Chart. Yes, Blues Boy Jones' song, "Come on Home", had been in fourth place on the Top 20 Chart and placed 43rd in the Top 100 Chart! People were selling Blues Boy Jones' old vinyl records universally on the Internet. I saw in Japan where they were advertising "Come on Home." It was written in Japanese and I had to make a copy of that just for proof. It was hard to believe.

The songs "The Birds is Coming," flipside to "That's Cuz I Love You", were recorded in New York in 1963, when the Alfred Hitchcock movie *The Birds* was a big hit at the movies. At one time, this record was selling for $350 on E-Bay and "Rock n Roll bells" was selling for $300. Now all of the prices varied over time. My father's music could be purchased on Amazon Music, eMusic, iTunes and many record companies worldwide.

Saturday, September 28, 2013, an article titled "A Blues Boy's International Legacy" hit the *Wharton-Journal Spectator*. Wharton is my hometown, so this was one of the greatest feelings ever. Family and friends told me that the article was well written. I told the editor, Ann Watson, that she nailed it and job well done.

On October 16, 2013, *Forward Times* newspaper of Houston, Texas featured an article on my dad. Here it was twenty-nine years later and my dad was featured in the *Forward Times* newspaper on the same page with pictures of Oprah and singer Robin Thicke. How cool was that!

The reason why I wanted the articles printed and contacted people who uploaded my dad's music was to get the word out there. I talked to as many people as I could about my dad's legacy because I wanted people to log onto the Internet and listen to Louis (Blues Boy) Jones and the Bobby Scott Orchestra's beautiful and timeless music that has been around for over fifty-eight years!

One follower of my dad's music stated that Jones never got his dues. When Pat (my stepmother) told me about a conversation that she and the late Selena Fulton had, I realized that my dad was a very dynamic and talented entertainer. Pat said that Selena told her about one night in Galveston when Louis was performing. The place was filled to capacity. So many people were packed in that place and there were just as many people standing outside waiting to come in to hear him sing.

My thoughts were that someone should make a movie about my dad's amazing life. I have heard so many wonderful things about my father's life. I believed there was much more yet to be discovered about him. However, some things will never be revealed.

In March 2013, I discovered more incredible news about my father. Someone uploaded a song called "I Believe to My Soul" written by the late Ray Charles on the Enjoy Record label and I was almost in a state of shock. A song written by the great Ray Charles! My father really sang this song.

Jamie Foxx did a great job singing this song in the movie *Ray*, but my dad did an awesome job! On the flipside of the song is a record called "Hurry Baby" written by Danny Robinson and the late Bobby Robinson, two brothers. Mr. Bobby Robinson was huge in the music industry. He owned several record labels and he was from New York.

The Internet has so much valuable information. One day in March 2013, I saw "Rock and Roll Bells" and it was located at the University of Mississippi in their Blues Archives. I called the university and contacted the museum curator Greg Johnson by e-mail. I informed Greg of who I was and asked if he would call me. Greg did call and he was happy to hear me. I told him about what was going on with my father's music on the Internet and he couldn't believe what he was hearing. Greg called me a few times and said to keep in touch with him about my dad's music. Another moment in history for Jones' music.

I am very happy and proud of my dad for the mark that he left in the music industry. It is such a great feeling to know that so many people respect him as an artist. I found on the Internet that my dad was featured in a newspaper, *The Billboard 100*. They had articles about his first song, "Rock n Roll Bells", and mentioned it quite often. A song titled "All Over, Goodbye" was on the flipside of Jones' first song, but it had not been uploaded on the Internet as of summer 2016.

Again, while browsing the Internet, I came across this story about a man named Scotty Moore. He had in his possession the late Elvis Presley's record collection. Hard to imagine, but this just sent me over the top. There was a list of twenty-six songs from the top artists in that time frame. Can you believe that one of Elvis' favorite songs was "Rock n Roll Bells", a song that was recorded by my very own dad? How amazing! All I could say was, "What's next to be discovered about my wonderful and talented father?"

The article went on to say that back on May 27, 2010, Mr. Moore sold Elvis' old record collection in London for over $75,000 dollars. Wow! I have enjoyed sharing all of these heartfelt stories about my father whom we loved and dearly miss. Hearing his voice through his music brings comfort to my aching soul. Music is an expression of love! Love was something that we shared. Dad, I thank you for sharing your beautiful gifts with the world. My brothers and I continued to search for the copyrights to our father's music. We appreciated each and every family member, friends (both new and old), his followers and his fans in places all around the world, for whatever they might have done to help keep Louis (Blues Boy) Jones' legacy alive.

Earlier in this story I mentioned that in December, 2011, Jones had about 2,000 views and his music had already been on the Internet since 2007 or perhaps longer. I was graciously grateful that people located in places all around this wonderful great big world still enjoyed listening to the sound of Blues Boy Jones. Drum roll please, as of November 2014, Jones has had over 89,499 total views and counting! He had had ten of his songs on the Internet. At the present time these songs are uploaded thirty-four different times from his followers in places worldwide! I applaud each and every one. I thank each of you from the bottom of my heart.

Meanwhile, Jeremy Pender, along with the help of so many people, was still working on getting a CD re-issued to pay tribute to Blues Boy Jones' music. We have been hoping to make this happen if all possible. It has been a long time coming but, to me it has been worth every second when it does happen.

Chapter 9

Memorable Moments and More

The school in which my father attended in his lifetime. The Old Central High School is now a cultural center. Can you imagine the thrill and excitement for my family, friends and I. On July 11, 2015 this is where I hosted my first book signing in honor of my Dad.

Louis Prince Jones Jr. attended Central High School. The school was located on 26th Street Avenue M in Galveston, Texas. The remodeled building now serves as a cultural museum for the community and visitors.

My mother said that my father was a good cook. We laughed because she said he thought that he made the best smothered chicken with rice and gravy in the world and if you didn't tell him that he did, you might have to kill him.

One summer my dad had made seafood gumbo. When I tasted it back then, and still remembering it today, there was none better. My oldest daughter LaRoysha was also a great cook and my brother Harold was a good cook. I do a good job cooking, but my dad had us all beat. He was the best cook.

My cousin Clifton O'Neal told me that my father was a great card and domino player. I had never known that before then. That explained why my siblings, my children and I liked to play cards and dominos almost every chance that we got when we had a gathering. It was always a lot of fun.

Cousin Phillip O'Neal Jr. told me that some years ago he and my father worked at a shipyard in Galveston. Phillip said that my dad was so funny telling jokes that it was hard for them to work. Philip said that my dad would have people laughing so hard that their tummies would start to ache. How funny I thought.

My mother resided in San Francisco, California. She remained somewhat bitter about being married to my father because of certain circumstances. In April 2012, while my mother was visiting me, I told her to come and listen to my dad's music on my computer. I tried to be a peacemaker, so I talked her into listening to my dad's music on YouTube. A priceless picture. The expression on her face brought tears to my eyes.

My mother said, "Vernie that's him. He still sounds good. After all of these years, I never thought that I would ever hear his voice again. He still can sing." My mother went on to tell about my dad and her going to hear Otis Redding perform at a Christmas Eve dance in Baytown, Texas in the early 1960s. She told me that Otis and my dad were good friends.

I said, "Aaw mama, you didn't tell me that before."

She said, "Oh, yes, they were good friends." Then she told me that singer Joe Tex was also a friend of my dad's.

Louise Frances Howard (Jones)

My mother is just as eloquent and beautiful then and now, age 78.

In the early 1950s and 1960s, these were some of the clubs that my father performed at in the Galveston area: The Jambalaya, Big Heavy's, and Club Manhattan.

My dad was the lead singer in two different bands. The first band was called "Louis Jones and His Band" and the other band was called "Louis (Blues Boy) Jones and the Bobby Scott Orchestra". Joe Smith gave me the names of the Bobby Scott band members. He said that a man who went by the name of Tunne started out playing the drums with them. Then after that, a guy named Hasson Meirer played the drums; he was from Pennsylvania. Patrick Williams, from Galveston, Texas, played the trumpet. Bobby Scott was from Houston, Texas, and he was on tenor saxophone with Malcolm Easter on trombone, and Joe Smith, from Brenham, Texas was the lead guitarist.

Joe Louis Smith, the last living band member of the Bobby Scott Orchestra. Blues Boy Jones was the lead vocalist. Joe played bass guitar, now age 78. He resides in Detroit, Michigan. Joe says he is still making beats.

My cousin Clifton O'Neal lived in Galveston and he wanted me to meet a man by the name of Lockie Edwards Jr. My cousin said Lockie and my father wrote songs together. This brightened my world that I was going to meet someone that worked with my dad in the music industry. Also, my cousin said that Mr. Edwards was known to have written songs for the "Queen of Soul", Aretha Franklin. I was very heartbroken because I did not get the chance to meet Lockie. My cousin did inform me about Mr. Edwards having some health issues. Sadly, he passed away January 13, 2012.

Recently, I read about this great entertainer on the Internet. Lockie wrote songs for the late Nat King Cole, Neil Diamond and many other giants is the music business. Lockie was truly a remarkable legend himself.

Back in April 2012, I spoke with a lady who worked at the Galveston Chamber of Commerce. When I shared the story about my father's legacy, the lady was so inspired that she told me this story about my father was one of the most amazing stories that she had heard in a very long time. I told her that I hoped one day the city of Galveston would name a street after my dad. The lady told me to get in touch with Casey Greene. He was Head of Special Collections and the Texas History Center at the Rosenberg Library for the city of Galveston.

When I shared the story with Casey, he told me that a story such as this needed to be shared with the people of Galveston. After all, this was one of the Island's very own. Casey said he would be delighted to share the information about Jones by placing him in the Vertical File at the library once he viewed all the material on my father. Casey said that people would be able to read about all the great history on a blues singer from Galveston, Texas.

In the beginning of March 2013, I took Casey Greene some information on my father. After Casey examined the material, by the end of March 2013, the information about Louis Blues Boy Jones' legacy was labeled in a folder with his name on it and placed in the Vertical File at the Rosenberg Library to share with people far and near.

Casey Greene sent me a letter stating, "Your father must have been very special." Another great act of kindness from Casey. I called Casey and thanked him for this grand opportunity on behalf of my father's music and legacy!

In March 2013, my friend Jen and I traveled to Galveston Island. I was constantly looking for people who remembered my dad and I have tried to locate many of his old friends. I came across a gentleman named John Santana and he told me that he once played the trumpet for the band. John said that they were young and while performing, sometimes the club would make $500 to $700 dollars a night, yet some of the band members were paid only $25 to $50 for each performance. John said that was a lot of money back then but, as young men, he said that they did a lot of partying and didn't know the business part of the music industry, nor did they have anyone to teach them.

He remembered them having an Italian man for their manager and he knew that they were not treated fairly. I showed him an old photo of my father and his first band. John knew some of the band members. He said that the alto saxophone player was a young man named Peewee; David was on tenor saxophone and Peanut on the drums. Other men that played for the band were Douglas McKinley, (now deceased) on bass guitar, and Eddie Wileby played guitar (deceased).

In the early seventies, I loved music and so I often tried to write songs. I wrote a song (lyrics) and I mentioned earlier how I loved listening to a radio station from Nashville. I found out that if you were a song writer, you could send your songs to this company and they would make a record for you. I was thinking that I could be like my dad — make a record and people would hear my song over the radio; I was so excited.

Making the record came with a price tag of $59.99, so I asked my Mother if she would give me the money to send to this record company; then I could have my very first record made.

My mother told me that it was a good idea but, she didn't have the money to spare. I was sad. Then my mother said to me, "I'll call your father and see if he will help you." I went on to explain to my dad that the company supposedly had reduced the price to only $19 dollars, and I could have a record made that was going to be played on several radio stations. I was so happy. I loved hearing my dad talk and I was even happier talking to him about a song that I had written called, "I Need Love".

My dad told me that what I had done was good, but he went to say, "LaVern, let me explain something to you." He said, "If you have something and it is good enough, don't worry, because if it's worth something, you don't want to have to pay them; they will pay you." I was a young teenager and until this very day I have never forgotten that quote from my dad. Truly words of wisdom, thanks Dad.

On December 21, 2013, I got another phone call from David Torkelson, owner of *The Galveston Wizard* or *G'Whiz* newspaper, which is a local newspaper in the Galveston, Texas area. I was introduced to David by a co-worker at my job by the name of Cindi Durrance. She was intrigued by the story about my father. Cindi told me she knew this great editor named David Torkelson. She had given David my telephone number about two months prior. Cindi said she knew David would be more than happy to feature Jones in his newspaper.

David did call me promptly. We had a great conversation. David said he would work on this project and got an article on my father's legacy ready for publication in his newspaper. I struggled to hold back my tears when David told me that my dad's article which I had written was going to be featured in his newspaper. I thanked David for making this wonderful opportunity possible. I was most grateful for this article, because Galveston was Jones' hometown and what a way to honor his legacy. I had tried for over a year to get some of the articles that I had written about Jones' life and his music to be featured in certain newspapers. Although, it took a longer period of time for some of the newspaper editors to agree to print these articles, I never gave up. Much appreciation to all of the great editors for a job well done on each article that has been printed so far. This has been another joyous moment for me and grand milestone for Blues Boy Jones' legacy!

I continued to wait anxiously and hoped for the day when The *Galveston Daily Newspaper* would print an article on my father. Perhaps I may get the opportunity to explain this statement in an interview one day; I continued to be hopeful.

On February 18, 2014, I received a telephone call from Mr. Leon Banks Jr., who lived in Galveston, Texas. Mr. Banks wanted to introduce me to a man who knew my dad well. He wanted me to talk with Joe (Bubba) Gilmore. Joe was a friend of my dad. I was crazy excited to talk to with Mr. Gilmore. Joe told me that he used to chauffeur my dad around to wherever he had to perform. Joe said my dad paid him $20 for each trip and with gas being only 15 cents a gallon. Joe said he thought he was rich. Joe and I laughed about this.

I had a lot of respect for Joe. He explained to me how some of the people were treated back then in the music business. Joe informed me that my dad was an international entertainer, yet my dad was cheated out of his earnings. He said during the time while in the music business, a contract was signed, but it was phony, not real. The manager would tear the papers up and throw the papers away, so there would be no record of a signed contract, as though it never existed. If you mentioned that you wanted to get a lawyer, the manager would tell you that you were too smart to need one and then the manager would find a way to get rid of you.

Joe said most of the time the manager provided you with gas money to travel to your next show. You got a meal or sometimes the manager would help you with clothing for a show. Joe said you were not going to get rich or have money saved in a bank account. The managers made the largest amount of all the earnings. The managers had leverage over the performers because they provided them with a car. Joe said a car was the most important thing in a person's life. A car, namely a Cadillac, meant high success. Joe said that you never paid for the car. The manager never told you how much the car cost, so you made payments for that car for a very long time through the manager.

My thoughts on this were: Very interesting information from someone who witnessed some of the down side of the music business. However, I must agree that many entertainers did achieve a great amount of success in the music business during that era.

Sean Courtney from Glasgow, United Kingdom requested my friendship on Facebook. He introduced me to a website called Rhythm & Blues Kingdom. This website displayed the music of many great artists in the early years. Some of the artists may have been forgotten or had gone unnoticed. I hope readers will check this website out. I enjoyed listening to all of the talented artists from long ago; that's what I call real music!

This amazed me: seeing all of the comments made by people who loved listening to my father's music. I had to hold back the tears. Sandra Hutchinson stated in the 1980s that the Blues Boy Jones' song "I'll Be Your Fool" was a big hit on the dance floor. She said that she had loved Jones' music ever since. Prettyboy Saverece said that my dad was a shining star in the Kingdom and they never stopped playing his music. Steve Pilkington said that he had loved my father's music with a passion ever since Sandra Hutchinson introduced him to Jones' incredible vocal prowess. Wow!

Back in 2012, one of his supporters stated that his music had caught on like wildfire! Blessed was what I was feeling. I thank each of you for appreciating my father's music and honoring his legacy on a level such as this. Truly, we have all been blessed by Louis Jones' phenomenal legacy.

I hoped for the people on Galveston Island to name a street after one of their very own. I was dreaming big because the story was not finished. Louis Blues Boy Jones is still Rockin' the Blues over 58 years!

Rockin' n Roll Bells/All Over Goodbye by Louis Jones and His Band, recorded on Peacock records in 1956. A rare priceless treasure for me to be holding my father's first recording. My kids and grandkids witnessed this great piece of history for our family. A once in a lifetime memory for all of us!

The second record I purchased of my dad's music, these two songs: "Rock n Roll Bells" and "All over Goodbye", were Jones' first recordings from the year 1956. What love and joy I felt in my heart just to be able to hold, and better yet, to listen to my father's music. Even greater news, these records were now in my possession and this perhaps was one of the greatest pieces of history ever in my lifetime! It was a dream come true. Shout out to all the record companies and music lovers around the world: Thank you for holding onto these lost pieces of treasure, Louis Blues Boy Jones' timeless music!

Memories in My Heart

Earlier in this book, I mentioned my Aunt Velma Ruth Langston, who was my mother's oldest sister. I will forever miss her beautiful smile. I never heard nor do I ever recall my Aunt Velma complain about anything. She had such a beautiful spirit. I will love her for an eternity. When Velma invited her sister Louise to Galveston, Texas that summer, this was the reason why I have this amazingly loving story to share with people in places all around the globe. The summer of 1952 will be cherished for a lifetime by many people because of Louis Prince Jones Jr., my dad, meeting Louise Frances Howard, my mother.

However, I was so broken hearted after receiving such devastating news once again. My Aunt Velma had suffered a stroke on December 24, 2013. My precious and loving Aunt Velma passed away February 23, 2014, at the age of 79.

Sadly my brother Harold Leonard Jones, Blues Boy Jones' second son, lost his battle to lung cancer on March 28, 2014. Dad called him Harold Baby. Rest my dearly beloved brother, rest...

On May 21, 2014, I contacted the Texas Historical Association by e-mail. I submitted a letter about Louis Blues Boy Jones. Editor Laurie Jasinski replied that the story about my father's life was very interesting. Laurie told me that she wanted to place my father in the *Texas History Handbook,* which is an online encyclopedia viewed by millions yearly. She explained that Jones would have more exposure for his legacy. Screaming and shouting, "Thank you, Laurie." She was an editor for seventeen years and a project manager with Texas History Association in New Braunfels, Texas. On August 26, 2014, Louis Blues Boy Jones from Galveston, Texas was placed into Texas History!

Also, Laurie told me that before the end of the year she would place Blues Boy Jones' music into the *Texas History Music Handbook*. My gratitude ran deep for Laurie because she informed me that the bio that I had written on my father in August 2013, was submitted by my cousin Phil O'Neal (Mookie). However, there was no positive feedback about the article. All of this time, the bio had just been sitting in limbo on Wikipedia. Laurie found the link to this bio while doing research on Jones.

Earlier in August 2014, I contacted Wikipedia for answers on what to do next about the article. I joined the talk section of Wikipedia to notify someone about a few changes or errors that needed to be corrected. Guy Hamilton replied. Guy told me that the articles were not concrete and my father's information was not notable for Wikipedia. Guy was a master editor from Chepstow, Wales. He had been working for more than eight years for Wikipedia. I respected Guy's title. I did not get upset by his reply. I thought to myself, *I am going to work a little harder and I will help my father become notable enough for Wikipedia.* I told Guy I would soon be publishing a book about Jones' life and that he was inducted into the *Texas History Handbook.* Guy e-mailed quickly and said for me to watch Wikipedia. On August 31, 2014, blues legend, Louis Blues Boy Jones from Galveston, Texas was officially placed on Wikipedia! What a huge accomplishment for my father's legacy. I thank you Guy Hamilton. Your kindest deed will never be forgotten.

On May 28, 2014, I received more hurting and terrifying news from San Francisco, California. My oldest brother Louis III had shortness of breath. He was rushed to the hospital. Louis was diagnosed with stage 4 lung cancer. We had not yet gotten over Harold. My mother's health also concerned us. We all felt helpless and our sense of direction was definitely off course and shaken. We immediately asked for prayers for our entire family. We were struggling daily trying to deal with such devastation and this heartbreaking news. We thanked God when Louis turned fifty-nine years old on August 11, 2014. He was in good spirits. Louis did not want to take Chemotherapy. We asked that people please keep us in their prayers. We prayed for a miracle and we humbly thanked everybody.

Louis Jones III was Blues Boy Jones'
oldest son and my dad called him Baby
Louis. Louis is holding Bryce
Hutchinson, his grandson in the picture.

**Elmira Frances Hutchinson (Louis'
daughter) and her daughter
Ki'Andra Hutchinson (Louis'
grand-daughter).**

Louis Hutchison (My brother,
Louis' son and father to Bryce.

Leelan Rashad Prince Jackson Jr.

On June 2014, to commemorate my father's 30th year since passing, I decided to do something special for Blues Boy Jones. I let my nine-year-old grandson pay a tribute to his great-grandfather's legacy by singing Jones' ten songs on YouTube. Leelan Rashad Prince Jackson Jr. did a terrific job! He sang a few lines of each song without music and only in one session. We were thankful for his bold spirit. At the time of this writing, Leelan had a total of 542 views and counting!

He was nine years old and in this photo Leelan had a lead part in his school play, called *BONES!* Leelan was portraying the late Elvis Presley. His character in the play was called Pelvis because he sang and danced like Elvis. It was so cool to watch. I couldn't help but think about my dad as a young man performing on many stages during his career. Leelan loved the stage. This was my son's child and my only grandson.

Leelan Rashad Prince Jackson Sr.
(my son). I wanted our family
name Prince to be carried on.

I held something within for many years. I had never laid eyes on my father's grave. I hurt and have cried often because of my father telling his last wife Pat that he had nothing to live for after losing his mother. I told Pat he had his children and grandchildren. I may never truly understand some things in life. I waited twenty-nine years before I recently shared this information with some family members about how I felt. I came to the conclusion that I had to respect my father's feelings; his mother was his everything. In life my father knew his mother was all he truly could depend on when life was uncertain.

I said, "I will not publish my book until I lay eyes on my father's grave." I still became emotional because I knew when I saw my Dad's grave, my emotions would be almost out of control. August 22, 2014, over thirty years later, my eyes beheld my father's grave for the very first time. Peaceful, as the wind blew upon my face. It was so peaceful. Thank you, God. Dad, I love you and you rest on peacefully. I am all right and I can move forward.

The pain of losing my father will never go away but I felt I overcame my fear of him being buried. My nine-year-old grandson while touching his great-grandfather's headstone said, "We miss you, Papa, and we love you." What comforting words from a child.

My beloved father's grave.

To me this moment, in my heart it felt like I was in the year 1984. Love never dies. But, pain after losing a love one someway, somehow; can still linger...

In September 2014, once again I contacted the city of Galveston about naming a street after my father for his contributions to the music industry. Liz Rogers and Janice Norman worked for this department. These two ladies got things rolling for me about the name change. I attended two hearings at the Galveston City Hall in October 2014. In the first hearing, the Galveston Planning Committee made the decision for a second hearing and to proceed with renaming a street after my father. People in the community were allowed to participate. One resident of the Island voted in favor of changing a street sign to LOUIS BLUES BOY JONES! Also, in the second hearing, Galveston Mayor Jim Yarbrough and six city Council members shouted. "Yes! A total of seven votes while in court, again unanimously in favor of the name change."

Some of the people on City Council made comments such as: "We saved the best for last." One man walked up to me and told me that he had not heard a story such as this in a long time; it was the coolest story and he would go home and listen to my father's music on YouTube. One lady told me that she could not wait to get home and share this good news with her husband because they grew up on this kind of music, blues music.

I chose this address because of the family history associated with that address. The house still stands. My grandmother, the late Rebecca Prince Jackson (Jones' mother), occupied this address for many years. In addition, my mother and my father once lived there when they were married. My two brothers and I spent countless summers there when we were young. My children and grandchildren have seen the house at this address. I have always loved to visit Galveston. It is such a beautiful Island and I have relatives who still live there. Many cherished and heartfelt unforgettable memories to last a lifetime happened at 909 37th Street for our entire family.

It wasn't long before the sign went up! Dad, you are not forgotten. People are already talking about visiting Galveston, Texas just to see Louis Blues Boy Jones' name. I was at a loss for words. People near and far have had so much respect for my father and they have wanted to honor Jones as one of the greatest artists who was finally getting his proper recognition. I was grateful to be advocating for such a man as this and he was my dad. Dad, this is for you. You deserve this and more. Louis Blues Boy Jones, Dad, your legacy and music will live on in our hearts for a lifetime, generation after generation!

In this photo, October 28, 2014, I was
being recorded live on G-TV,
Galveston's Municipal Television
Channel 16, it's a local TV channel in
Galveston, Texas. This was the actual
hearing in which the final decision was
made (six unanimous in favor of, plus
the Mayor and with the one outside
vote, an overall total of eight Islander's
voting) to rename 909 37th Street, Louis
Blues Boy Jones! Mr. Leon Banks Jr. and
my oldest daughter LaRoysha Jackson
Walker attended this grand occasion
with me for support. Yet, I was so

nervous.

Ian Goodrum was an editor of *The Facts*, a newspaper in Clute Texas. On Sunday, November 2, 2014, Louis Blues Boy Jones was on the front page! History set again. The article was titled: REDISCOVERY NEW GENERTION ENRAPTURED BY THE VOICE OF LOUIS JONES. 'BLUES BOY IS BACK'. Ian talked about the obscure Texas singer earning newfound popularity in the Internet age! This article was at the top and was, no doubt, ground-breaking history for my father's legacy! Ian, you are a phenomenal editor and I thank you for your greatness.

When I called Ian up to thank him personally, he told me that a lot of stories come along but this particular story about my father was one that needed to be shared and it was a pleasure for him to write this article. I had to catch my breath so tears would not flow. I was just overwhelmed with all the respect for my father's legacy. What a great moment in time for all of us!

On November 12, 2014, I had much respect for Alfonso Bonmati, known as DJ Fonsoul. Sir, I thank you kindly for spinning Blues Boy Jones' records for his fans to enjoy! Fonsoul is a traveling DJ serving up early 1950s Rhythm & Blues to late 1970s Disco Soul music in Barcelona, Spain and many places around Europe. Fonsoul is a record collector and he shared this information with me on YouTube: he owns four of my father's old vinyl records. This totally blew my mind! Also, I would like to send a special shout out with a huge thank you to all of the DJs around the globe. Keep playing great music for the world to enjoy!

This is a letter from one of my Dad's good friends. I thank God for our acquaintance and I thank my dear friend Jeremy Pender. Mrs. Verdell Mack Sanders has shared many great stories about what life was like for my dad and her during their music careers. She is the co-writer for the song titled The Birds is Coming. This song was written in 1963 while they lived in New York City and was recorded on the Decca record label. What History!

Then Mrs. Sanders finally provided me with information on how they met boxer Cassius Clay in Florida one year. While Jones and his band was on tour. They stayed at the same hotel with Clay. She told me that he was very friendly and talked about things concerning life with them. What an honor! Mrs. Verdell now resides is West Virginia Beach, Virginia. We keep in touch by phone calls and emails. She is a jewel.

LaVern,

I rejoice with you!!
May God forever Bless you for keeping
your daddy's legacy alive.
Your father was a great musician and
most importantly he was a happy
man. Whenever I saw his face
regardless of how I felt 'I SMILED'.
This honor IS truly a blessing to all
who had the pleasure of his 'RAW'
soul sound and the WARMTH of his
SMILE.

THANK YOU LaVern FOR KEEPING
THE LIGHT SHINING.

WARMEST REGARDS,

VERDELL

Also, my Uncle Andrew and Cousin David shared with us how my father took two pictures with the boxer Clay. Jones was in the army. Cousin David often tell us about the time my father had lunch with Cassius Clay. My dad was very comical. David says they all laughed when my father said. "He didn't see any pork chops on the menu". Unfortunately, someone took the two photographs of my dad and this world known boxer from my Uncle's photo album. So sad, I didn't get the chance to lay my eyes upon these rare pictures.

CHAPTER 10

What Happened Next

Finally, after I had written all the amazing things that I wanted people to know about my dad, I traveled to many locations talking with family and friends. I had a constant desire in my heart to seek for more information that others might know about Louis (Blues Boy) Jones. I have attended numerous book signings for *The Re-Introduction of a Blues Legend* — the first version of my book. In my heart I knew this story was not over. In my mind I often wondered what would be next in recording my father's life and career during the years he was in the music industry.

People of all ethnic groups were still viewing and uploading his music on YouTube. Jones' old vinyl records were still being purchased in all parts of the world. He story had appeared in many newspaper articles and there was an article about Jones in a magazine located overseas.

I had keep moving forward trying to connect with someone to help me reach that goal of which I had spoken about nine years before. I wanted a movie created from the story of my dad's life. So I needed a script writer. Then I needed a movie director/producer. I had been working diligently for this cause. I knew all things were possible. I believed by faith things would work out. Maybe Jones' movie would win several awards. Hey! I was dreaming big.

One thing I did believe in was that all things happened for a reason. My first book signing was on Saturday, July 11, 2015. I wanted the book signing to be something special and memorable. It was held at the Old Central School in Galveston, Texas. During his lifetime, my father attended this very school. I wanted to honor my dad because this was all about his legacy. Galveston was my first choice to have a book signing since the island was the hometown of Blues Boy Jones.

It was a good turn out as far as family and friends were concerned. People looked on amazed at all of the memorabilia that I had on my dad. I truly enjoyed the conversations with each person. Lots of photos were taken and everyone seemed to be having a great time. I would never forget this one photo that captured my heart every time I looked at it. It was the photo of my granddaughter looking at her great grandfather's pictures.

This photo of Rylee Walker (Jones'
seven-year-old great-granddaughter) is
such a heart touching photo and still
brings tears to my eyes. A look of love.

I had to go back a few years ago to talk about what happened next for Louis Prince Jones Jr. In 2012, I made a phone call to the Galveston Chamber of Commerce. I told the lady all that was going on with my dad's music and legacy. I remember telling her this, "One day I hope the people of Galveston will name a street after him and I would like for them to set aside a day to honor my dad for his contributions to the music industry. My father loved his hometown."

Then she replied, "And they should; he was a native of the island and this is an amazing story."

I shouted with joy. Just knowing a stranger on the other end of the phone had that much compassion for my father. Earlier in this book, there were pictures of the street signs. I attended two hearings in October 2014, at the Galveston City Hall where I heard a total of seven unanimous votes of, "Yes". I was told one outside participant did cast his vote (yes) in favor of renaming the street sign. Mayor James Yarbrough signed the papers and allowed me to pick a street to be renamed Louis Blues Boy Jones. I chose the address: 909 37th Broadway.

My grandmother, the late Rebecca Prince Jackson (Jones' mother) resided there for many years. Also, in the past my two brothers and I would spend our summer vacations there with our grandmother Rebecca. My mother and my father lived there when they first got married. What a huge honor the islanders allowed for one of their natives. Never would I forget such generosity and kindness.

I thought there would be only one street named after my father, but 909 37th Sealy, located right across street, has been renamed after Jones, also. I hoped everybody, when traveling to this beautiful island, would please drop by and view a piece of history dedicated to Louis Blues Boy Jones!

The Street Signs Are Up! Galveston Island (Galveston, Texas)

Louis Blues Boy Jones 909 37th Broadway

Louis Blues Boy Jones 909 37th
Sealy

Great appreciation goes out to my best friend. Thanks for admiring the street sign renamed after my father.

CHAPTER 11

Another Author's Help

Sometimes in life things are hard to explain. My wondering mind was acting up again. I wanted to know how would I be able get my books available for purchase in stores such as Kroger, H.E.B, Wal-Mart, and other business places. I was a newcomer to writing and publishing and I was not ashamed to ask for help or advice from a person with more experience concerning any matter.

I made several phone calls each day and I left plenty of messages on the answering services with hopes of someone calling me back. At times I had spoken with the manager of a store or sometimes customer service representatives. I was at a standstill and with very little help on getting the first edition of my story on any store shelf. My book was available for on-line orders through Xlibris Publishing, Barnes and Noble on line, and Amazon. I did have some book signings to sell my own material. But in order for me to have more exposure, I knew I had to promote my book, which I was delighted to do. My journey had been more than amazing! It brought me great pleasure to constantly thank each individual for their loyal support.

While leaving a church service back in July 2015, my cell phone rang. I started not to answer the call because it was after 6 o'clock and the number was not familiar. Instead, I did take the call and on the end of the line was a lady who prefers not to be named directly. A few days earlier I had left a message on her voice mail. Prior to this I had spoken with another grocery store representative who told me that this woman was in charge of a special program for regional authors which I wanted to apply for. We got acquainted. The woman told me she was out of state on vacation. I told her to please call me back. I could wait until she returned to Texas. I did not want to disturb her family's vacation.

She insisted that she was going to be on vacation longer, but she was still "working". We decided on a short talk and I told her the reason for my telephone call, which was that I hoped to have that first version of the book sold in larger businesses like that grocery chain. She told me that she would be more than happy to assist me on getting my book into the chain's database for me to sell during book signings at regional stores. She was the coordinator of that program. She told me there were strict guidelines, yet she was willing to help me. She thought the story about my father's life sound like a great story. Also, she believed the book would do well in their stores.

What an evening! I was at church and this woman was on vacation out of state. Yet, we connected. A great beginning for both of us. We ended the phone call and I was instructed to give her a call back the following Monday for more details.

She and I continued to communicate by phone calls and emails. She wanted me to mail her one of my books. She had to make sure my book was appropriate for the store once she read it. After viewing my book, she told me that I needed to make changes to the text. I remember her saying, "This is a good story about your father and I believe it will do well in the stores. But there are a lot of mistakes in the text."

I agreed, because I felt like this was a chance some people may never get. Then she wanted to set up a date for us to meet and further discuss how that book program worked.

We met at a location that was good for both of us because of the distance between our homes. A friendship was bonded from the first phone call. Meeting this woman in person was like seeing one of my old friends. We talked about our families and we chatted about some of the latest happenings in the news. We had a good time while talking business. Things were looking good.

Most people told me that my story was good, so why change it? And remember earlier I mentioned that I had talked with a script writer. Some people told me that if you planned to turn the book into a movie, let the script writer make the necessary changes.

After contemplating several times over whether or not to let this woman edit and correct my story, I told her to let me wait at least one year. She was truly supportive and she respected my decision.

In the meantime, I informed my new friend about two more books that I had written. One book was about my ten-year-old grandson Leelan Jackson Jr.'s life and the other book was about relationships. I asked her if she would look at these two books for the grocery store program.

She said, "Sure." Everyone, my new friend was a noted published author of several dynamic books in circulation worldwide. She was a woman of integrity. She was full of wisdom and did not mind sharing her expert advice to help a cause.

What a year it was for me in 2015! Three published books available online with Amazon, Barnes and Noble and Xlibris. My new friend line edited these two books for me titled: *Give Him an Audience, Give it Your All.* The story is about my grandson's life. Meet Leelan Jackson Jr., he is the co-author of *Give Him an Audience.* He has done so many wonderful things in life educationally and biblically. You would be amazed!

I believe some people seek to find a soulmate in life: that special someone who will be around through the good times and the worst of times. *Missteps, Good Steps in Learning to Live: Tears, Faith & Love* is something for adults. I tried to capture the essence of finding Mr. or Mrs. "Happy Ever After". I believe he or she does exist.

I was still waiting on a movie deal on the story of my dad, Louis Prince Jones Jr., also known as Louis (Blues Boy) Jones. I have always loved and missed you, Daddy. I have always felt your halo.

CHAPTER 12

Two Proclamations

I've often wondered how a person would feel if there was a day named in their honor of them for something he or she had accomplished in life, or a subject a person was affiliated with in the past or present. Most of the time when a thought like this entered my mind, I started seeking advice from any source necessary until I got an answer. My Uncle Andrew often said to me, "Niece, you don't take the word no from anyone or you want stop until the person say, yes." Love my uncle Andrew.

One day I decided to make a telephone call to the Galveston City Hall. I needed advice on how I would go about getting a day named after Louis Blues Boy Jones for his contributions to the music industry. I spoke to a lady by the name of Rose D'Ambra. I told Rose my father was a native of Galveston. She replied, "I will email you the form. Fill it out and return it to me." I thought that seemed pretty simple. All I had to do was fill out the form and send it back. This was in July 2015.

Most of the time, I don't get in a hurry. I liked to spend a small amount of time meditating over whatever I was dealing with before I made a final decision to move forward. I wanted to make the best choice on any subject and feel good about it. Besides this was my dad. Although, he was no longer alive, I still had the upmost respect for him and his legacy. Also, I was sharing this information with the world.

After receiving the email from Rose, I started filling in the information because there was a guideline included for me to follow. I carefully filled in the blanks about my father's life and his accomplishments to the best of my knowledge. On August 10, 2015, I decided to submit the proclamation to Rose. She quickly emailed me back with instructions to list the information on my father from the most important to the least important. She said the information was a little lengthy. Rose explained to me in one of the emails that if she could use all of the information that I had submitted, she would. However, she might not be able to fit everything on the form.

Praying is something often I do. August 11, 2015, was a glorious day for my family, Jones' followers, friends and I to celebrate. I was thanking Rose through an email for the mere fact that she took time out of her busy day to submit a proclamation form to me. I had to let Mrs. D'Ambra know that I was feeling grateful for her kind deed. Before I sent my email, I noticed Rose had sent another email back to me. I must admit that I was a little puzzled. So, I got in a hurry that moment to read Rose's email. Tears and screams of thankful joy! Rose said in her email that the mayor would sign the proclamation naming a day for my father that day!

Oh! My God! There were words of silence. Can you imagine something that I spoke about four years before was now a dream come true. Then Rose emailed me back and said the mayor had left the building. But she would get him to sign the form by that Thursday.

What a day in history for Louis Prince Jones Jr.'s family! Mayor James Yarbrough from the City of Galveston signed the Proclamation stating Louis Prince Jones Jr. Day will be declared on Galveston Island starting April 28, 2016! Again moments of silence as I tried to grasp the joy I was feeling inside. Thanking my dad first because he left a legacy behind that I felt needed to be recognized. With a humble heart I thanked everyone. This was another huge accomplishment for me as well. I looked forward to having as many people as possible come out on that day.

Backing up a bit, in September 2015, I got another email from Rose. She wanted to know when I was coming to the Island to pick up my Proclamation. She had it waiting for me. I told Rose that I was still excited. I explained to her that I worked four days a week out of town. But soon as I got a break, I would come to Galveston. By October 2015, I still had not made it to the Island. We were quite busy in the month of October because of my husband's Pastoral Anniversary.

November 13, 2015, my husband and I finally made it to the island. I couldn't believe how nervous I was as I approached the office looking for Rose. We connected right way. The atmosphere was very friendly for both parties. Emotionally, I started crying when Rose submitted two Proclamations to me.

She said, "One for your father and one for your grandson." What a surprise! I looked at Rose a little confused about the Proclamation for my grandson, Leelan Jackson Jr. Rose told me that it was because of what my grandson was doing. He seemed to be following in his great grandfather's footsteps with his own singing. The mayor thought it was fitting for Leelan to have a Proclamation from the City of Galveston as well.

As I held the two Proclamations in both hands, my dad was on my mind along with my ten-year-old grandson. Leelan was at school. My heart rejoiced with gratefulness. Sometimes, I believe saying thank you is not enough. But when spoken from the heart, it truly is.

We continually thanked Mayor James Yarbrough, Rose D'Ambra, the islanders and everyone around the globe for supporting my dad, Louis (Blues Boy) Jones' legacy!

Leelan could not believe that he had a Proclamation with his name on it. We were thrilled about everything. Leelan was thankful that Mayor Yarbrough acknowledged him since Leelan had always enjoyed singing. We hoped everyone would view him on YouTube singing his great grandfather's ten songs. Leelan paid a tribute to his great grandfather and my dad in those videos. Grandson, we were proud of you!

Often in my mind, heart and soul, I felt my daddy's loving spirit with a beautiful smile on his face shining down us from above...

Two Proclamations

Rose and one speechless smiling lady.

Leelan and his first Proclamation from
the Mayor of Galveston Island.

CHAPTER 13

Book to Movie

In the summer of 2015, we attended the wedding of a couple who were members of our church. I met the daughter of the groom. This young lady sang at the wedding. She had a beautiful voice. I had to meet this young lady and congratulate her on the gift of singing. She was very kind. I told her about my father's legacy. She told me how proud she was of my accomplishment as an author. When I told Jameshia Bankston about how I hoped to have my book turned into a movie one day, she told me that she was an actress, also. And she had appeared in a few small films. That was being at the right place and time for both of us. I liked the fact that this young lady gave me some good advice concerning business matters.

Jameshia told me about a man by the name of Norman Ray Fitts. She believed Norman could help me reach my goal of turning my book into a movie and for me to view his profile over the Internet. This caught my attention because the statement I made in October 2007 was, "I hope one day someone will make a movie," talking about a movie on my dad's life. We agreed to keep in touch by email and phone calls when possible. I thanked Jameshia and gave her my best regards on her career as an aspiring actress. Also, Jameshia told me that she made an appearance in one of Norman's films. She said the next time she came in contact with Norman she would mention me.

I viewed his profile over the Internet and found that Norman Ray Fitts was an Assistant Organizer for The Houston Film Industry Meetup Group located in Houston, Texas. Mr. Fitts was a world known writer, novelist, screenwriter, creative writing instructor and had many other talents. After sending a few emails to Norman, I finally got a reply from him. We did not waste time. I shared with him the information about my book. He told me right away that from the information that I had given him about my father, was something he might want to be involved in. I was just honored to be talking to a man with as many qualifications in the film industry as Norman had.

When Norman decided to send me a contract on the specifics of turning my book into a script, I thought this could be it. The story of my dad's life on the big screen. But, I must confess my thoughts were, "God I need guidance. Is this something I really want to do at this time? Am I ready?" Contemplation overload. I had the contract in my hand. I was ready to have a lawyer view the contract. The highlight of that one night in August 2015, was when Norman Ray Fitts gave me a phone call. We had the best conversation. Norman shared knowledgeable information with me on business matters. We enjoyed talking about our personal lives on subjects such as our marriages and grandkids. He shared this joke about Norman being normal. We both laughed. Then Norman wanted to meet and discuss the script contract and fee.

All night I wrestled with making a decision to sign or not sign. In my mind I wanted to, but in my heart I was not ready. I cancelled everything until I felt the moment was right. I wanted this movie to be just as amazing as my father was to me. I do have plans to contact Norman again. However, I figure if not Norman Ray Fitts, then it will be someone else. I believe God will direct my path. Time will tell and one day, the story of my dad's life might be in a theater near you! Again, I have always dreamed BIG!

CHAPTER 14

Marked Unknown

I still continued searching, wanting to know more about my dad's life. The Internet had been a giant source of help ever since I had been advocating for my father's legacy. At the start, few people knew about the life of a traveling musician from Galveston, Texas. In the beginning there was very little information known about blues singer, Louis Prince Jones Jr. Now, the Internet and people around the globe know more than ever about this legendary singer.

Let me share this incident. First, we have to go back and then come up to date to what was going on for this mind-blowing and tearful yet gratifying piece of information. Are you ready?

In one of my other books, my grandson, Leelan Jackson Jr., was chosen to sing with a five-piece band. Leelan and I met entertainer and host Bobby Reed. Mr. Reed was a known entertainer who hosted yearly music events in the area where we live. When Bobby asked Leelan if this was something he wanted to participate in, Leelan said to me, "Nana I want to sing at this event."

I told him that he could. He had to submit seven songs to Bobby. He picked three songs out of the seven for each participant(s) to sing. Many of our family and friends were excited for something as mega as this. Having a family member that was going to be on stage with a live band. Wow! What next?

Leelan R. Prince Jackson Jr.

Leelan singing and rapping.

Leelan had about two months to practice the songs. "Rock n Roll Bells" by Louis Jones and His Band, "I Can only Imagine" by Mercy Me, and "Never say Never" by Justin Bieber featuring Jaden Smith. Just think, so many years before, my dad was on stage singing "Rock n Roll Bells", his very first song that was recorded on Peacock records in 1956. Now, Jones' ten-year-old great-grandson, Leelan Jr. had been given an opportunity to make us proud.

I shopped for Leelan's attire, making sure he dressed the part. He had black Stacy Adam shoes, black tuxedo pants, black bow tie and a white tuxedo shirt. He was ready.

Leelan's debut to perform with a live band was on Saturday October 3, 2015, in Brazoria County. But something imaginable happened on Friday night October 2, 2015. I was making sure Leelan practiced his material. While checking on his wardrobe, I got a telephone call from my oldest daughter, LaRoysha Jackson. She had some exciting news for me to look into.

My daughter told me that it was rare for her to turn her television on in her bedroom. She was a busy working Mom. But she turned her TV on that night. When watching the news, she called me in a hurry and said, "Mom, you need to check out something that I just saw on the news. The University of Houston is hosting a Duke-Peacock event this weekend at the University." She knew that her grandfather did his first recording with Peacock records. I told her once I finished helping her nephew Leelan get situated with everything, I would look into what she had seen on the news. A few hours later, I called my daughter back for more information. LaRoysha told me all I had to do was log onto the U of H Digital Archives and Special Collections. I thanked my daughter and proceeded with this information.

But all this time while doing this for Leelan, my father was on my mind. I logged onto the information about the Duke-Peacock Archives. It was sheer joy seeing all the great entertainers photographs such as B. B. King, Little Richard, Bobby Blue Bland, Percy Sledge, Jr. Parker, Gate Mouth Brown, Buddy Ace and the list went on. I was happy, except deep within my heart. I was still searching for a picture of my own father. I said out loud, "Dad where are you?" Then my thoughts were: This is where you begin, Daddy. Why is there not a picture of you?

I came across this tiny photo marked "Unknown (possibly Carl Van Moon)". Immediately, I thought, "I don't know who Carl Van Moon is." So, I continued to look at more photos. But, something in my spirit told me to go back and look closer at the photo marked "Unknown". As I scrolled back to the picture, I blew it up to make it larger.

I started screaming with tears rolling down my face, "Daddy! Daddy! This is my Daddy!" I remember saying out loud, "I'm sorry Mr. Carl Van Moon I don't know who you are. But with no disrespect, this is my daddy, Louis Blues Boy Jones!"

Then I got in a hurry to notify the University of this finding. I also had to call my dear daughter LaRoysha back and thank her again for turning her television on that night. What a great discovery for our family! A priceless treasure.

I sent three emails to Special Collections. I notified a young man by the name of Matt Richardson. I wanted to call the University but, Mondays are so busy at my job, I had to wait until Tuesday, which is one of my days off.

When I called and spoke with Matt, He said, "We were going to call you. That is your father and we are going to change it to your father's name immediately."

Can you imagine the excitement for us? Over the weekend, I submitted a few details and other information via emails to the university about what was going on with Jones' music. Matt told me that he and Curator Vince Lee looked over my material and decided that the picture was definitely my father.

Matt said to me, "Vince will be calling you next." Both men were excited about this wonderful news. When Vince called me, we had the most amazing conversation. These men were so happy for me and the fact that my daughter led me to the U of H website. I still shed a few tears because of this one photo that was marked "unknown" for all those years now had a sense of life. My dad's sprit would live on in the hearts of many. I'd like to give a big shout out to Andrew Brown, who donated that picture of my father to the University's Special Collections department. Simply amazing! God bless you, and thank you sir!

Within a few days and email arrived in which Matt invited my grandson Leelan and me to the University of Houston. Vince and Matt wanted to meet us. I thought, "What a cool idea." We started making preparations to attend the M. D. Anderson Library Special Collections on the University Houston Campus.

Before setting a date to go to the U of H Library, I asked Matt and Vince what materials I could take to them for viewing pertaining to my father's music. I wanted to make sure it was safe to bring such items as photos, books and newspaper articles.

We got everything squared away on both ends and set a date for Saturday, January 30, 2016. Upon our arrival at the campus, my husband, our grandson Leelan, a friend of my husband by the name of Samuel Wilkes, and I were all greeted with a warm and a most friendly welcome. I was a bit nervous. But, in minutes because of Vince and Matt, I felt at home. We had so much fun sharing information from both parties. Vince and Matt let me take the floor to talk about my father and share the exhibit I had on Louis Prince Jones Jr. These two gentlemen were surprised at all the information I had on my dad.

Then it was time for us to see the collection of the late Don Robey of Duke-Peacock records — the donated material from Andrew Brown. I just wanted to look at the picture of my dad that was once marked unknown. Vince started from the beginning showing us all the pictures of some of the greatest entertainers in the world: B. B. King, Bobby Blue Bland, Buddy Ace and more. There were several pages of Duke-Peacock book keeping records and lots of copies from some of the artists' old royalty checks. Quite interesting.

There was a moment of silence as I starred at the one large (8x10) negative. This photo that was in this scrap book on my dad. Can you imagine how I felt? That was why in my heart I believed there was more to come about this blues singer from Galveston, Texas. The story was not over.

Once a negative photo marked
UNKNOWN!

Vince (on the right), Matt (on the left) and I made an agreement to keep in touch of any new developing stories on Jones' legacy or music.

Photos while visiting the University of
Houston M. D. Anderson Special
Collections Library. This Campus is
located in Houston, Texas.

59 years later, my grandson and I holding some old checks with the signatures of the late Don Robey who owned Duke Peacock records!

CHAPTER 15

Lillian King Gobert

On February 17, 2016, I spoke with Lillian King Gobert. I mentioned Lillian earlier. She was a good friend of my late Aunt Velma R. Langston. Velma was my mother's oldest sister. These two ladies and my mother lived in Galveston, Texas, one summer and that's how my mother met Louis P. Jones Jr.

I knew Lillian was from Wharton, Texas. This was our home town. One night my mother and I were talking. She said to me, "Vernie, why don't you call Lillian up. She was your father's best friend and she may be able to tell your more things about him." Now I was stunned with enthusiasm. If anyone mentions something about my father, they have my attention.

My mother told me that Lillian was married to one of my dad's best friends named Henry Gobert. I remembered there had been several times my mother spoke about these two very good looking brothers, the Goberts.

Oh! What a time Lillian and I had talking about those days long ago. Right away Lillian said, "I just want to ask you one thing. Can you sing?"

"No, I'm sorry. That wasn't passed down to me." We both laughed so hard. I told Mrs. Lillian that my oldest daughter and my grandchildren sing, but I love to write.

Mrs. Gobert was eighty-five years old at that time. A Registered Nurse who resided in California told me when she retired, her plans were to move back home. We planned to keep in touch and when she had a chance to travel to Wharton, we were going to talk more about the friendship that she and my dad shared.

She said, "Your father and I were very close and we all had some good times together." Lillian told me how in love my father was with my mother. Also, how talented and smart my father was.

She even told me about the time when my daddy worked as a mortician's helper at the Stroud Funeral Home there in Galveston. "Singing was his greatest asset," said Lillian, "and your father was the best."

I can't explain the feeling in my heart when Lillian told me this, "Your father made Galveston a lot of money. He would bring in large crowds of people from the surrounding areas." Then she told me Louis, Henry and she were good looking and the clubs would not open their doors until they arrived. Wow! That's clout.

Lillian was looking forward to meeting me. She hoped to find some material that she had in storage pertaining to my dad and said she would bring it on her next visit to Texas.

Jones is smooth on this photo. What a beautiful smile on my Dad's face. Oh! How I wish I knew where this picture was taken. My Uncle Andrew gave me this photo of his baby brother. Thanks Uncle.

CHAPTER 16

Book Signings, Newspapers and Radio

The greatest joy for me has been meeting all of the beautiful people. My journey from the start had been so remarkable and at times it was hard for me to define a word that supported the level of happiness that I felt inside me. I have attended numerous book signings and have been delighted and grateful as I've traveled to each signing and interview. The people have been so loving and respectful. Countless times, I have met and greeted people of all ages and backgrounds, and it has been mind-blowing when Jones' followers tell me what an amazing story I have presented about my father. I smiled when his fans said, "Let us know when the movie comes out." It brought me so much gratification knowing that my dad's life story has touched the lives of many people universally.

There had been more front page appearances in newspapers for my family. In December 2015, my grandson and I graced the front page of *The Facts Newspaper*. This paper was published in Brazoria County. They had often sent out a shout-out newspaper editor, Mary Newport, and photographer, Sarah Rencurrel. I have thanked them for this privilege and told them, "You ladies rock as news reporters!" Leelan and I have been totally satisfied at the chance for such a privilege as this. What a very special moment in history for the Jones family.

I have also given thanks to some of the greatest librarians ever. We would forever appreciate three dynamic ladies at the *Wharton Journal-Spectator* down in Wharton, Texas: Curator Elene Gedevani, Assistant Director Beth Fain, and Mary Cervenka. In the summer of 2015, I called the library and told Beth about the first edition of my book. Beth asked me to come by the library because they wanted to meet me and view the book on my father. It was so kind of them, and I was looking forward to this trip, since Wharton is home for me.

Jones has been featured in several newspapers in the United States. Also, there was an article written about the man and his music in a blues magazine from the United Kingdom.

Beth and I met. We really connected and Beth asked me if I would please come to the Wharton Library during Black History Month in February 2016, and tell my story. Of course I said, "Yes," with no hesitation. This was home and I wanted to do this for my dad and my family. It was a good feeling, and I was blessed when somebody appreciated my hard work or good deeds. I was most humble about this invitation. I was close to sixty years old at that time, and I was having the time of my life, loving each moment.

Recently, Vince Lee spoke over live radio about my father, my first book *The Re-Introduction of a Blues Legend*, which is now replaced by this volume. He mentioned my husband and grandson. Vince sent me an email prior to this and told me that he was going to be on KPFT 90.1 FM. This radio station was located in the Houston, Texas. The segment on the show was called "Open Forum" and, if given the opportunity, he wanted to share the story on how we became acquainted. I was feeling so thankful. I was sure blessed with some of the most amazingly, friendly and caring people. That radio segment was about an hour long and the station covered a wide range.

Vince talked about the Duke-Peacock collections that Andrew Brown donated to the University of Houston. He said Andrew was a noted historian from the Houston area. Vince told me that Andrew was then up in age and he wanted to find a safe place for the record company's archives (Duke-Peacock).

When it was Vince's turn to speak, I made sure that I was listening. I was driving to work. I'm sure people didn't understand what was going on with me. After Vince talked about Don Robey, Gate Mouth Brown, B. B. king and others, it was Louis Blues Boy Jones' turn. When Vince said, "Shout out to LaVern. I know she is listening." I cried. I felt like I had received an award. What an honor for me hearing something of this magnitude coming from such a humble and very thoughtful friend! Thank you, Vince, thank you.

CHAPTER 17

Celebrate 4/28!

We were preparing to celebrate a blues legend's life. The event was scheduled to be held on Galveston Island, honoring Louis Prince Jones Jr., born April 28, 1931. His parents were the late Rebecca Prince Jackson and Louis Jones. His mother was from Brazoria, Texas. There was no information on his biological father. Jones was raised by his late stepfather, Charlie Jackson from Crockett, Texas.

Two sisters, Taneshia and I. Our hearts will forever be a part of Galveston Island!

When Mayor James Yarbrough signed the Proclamation allowing Louis Blues Boy Jones to be recognized for his contributions to the music industry, I shouted with joy! Thanks Galveston Islanders for participating and being some of the greatest supporters ever for one of your own. Mayor Yarbrough signed the Proclamation in August 2015! April 28, 2016, had been proclaimed "Louis Blues boy Jones Day" in Galveston, Texas. Jones would have been 85 years old. He was missed immeasurably. A day to remember. A time to celebrate.

I thanked each person for caring and standing by me on this marvelous journey and legacy about Blues Boy Jones.

People globally continued to honor and respect my father's contributions to the music industry. His ten songs were sweeping across the Internet. His music was uploaded by people from many countries and diverse backgrounds.

My thanks and gratitude for each of you is continuous!

There are some future plans and dreams for Jones' legacy and music. Laurie Jasinski had been working hard to place my father's music in the *Texas Music History Handbook,* an online encyclopedia. Laurie was a member of the Texas Historical Association. I continued to seek a script writer and movie director for the untold story of my father. I will keep everyone updated via Facebook, Twitter and my email address: lavern.lemons@yahoo.com

Love, peace and MUSIC!
God bless all...

Mr. Leon Banks & I

My very first book signing was held on Saturday, July 11th, 2015. When I called Mr. Banks up and offered him a ride. He told me, "No." "I'm going to walk. I'll be there." We both laughed. The old Central School is just a few steps from his home. Even with his illness, he found the strength to come support his friend. I will forever be grateful for his loving, respectful and caring friendship.

In remembrance of my dear friend Mr. Leon Banks. We shared many precious moments about my Dad. I would continue to miss his phone calls, the lovely inspirational cards he would send me and his wisdom. But, most of all I would miss my friend to the end. That was what Mr. Leon would tell me, "We're friends to the end." Rest now my dear friend. Love you. Mr. Leon lost his battle to cancer On October 31, 2015. I'll never forget what a kind spoken gentleman he was.

CHAPTER 18

From Unknown Photo to Known WORLDWIDE!

Since I have been advocating for my father's legacy, whether by emails, Facebook, phone calls, YouTube and numerous websites in all parts of the world, followers of Louis Prince Jones Jr.'s music were continually uploading his ten songs and making comments. Some of the comments were written in other languages. These left me in awe. Jones' old vinyl records were selling in places such as Japan and others listed below. I showcased two articles written in Japanese for people to witness at my book signings. I purchased the record "Come on Home" by Louis Blues Boy Jones with the Bobby Scott Orchestra from the United Kingdom.

What great pleasure it was for me hearing from a lady in Australia by the name of Monica Luppi saying how the twenty and thirty year olds were dancing to my father's music.

Then In Barcelona, Spain DJ Fonsoul sent me a message that he spins my Dad's records in the clubs over there.

In the United Kingdom another lady said that in the clubs, there the DJ's are playing Blues Boy Jones' music to a disco beat.

I was shocked when I read a comment from a man from the Galapagos Islands. That's way off the coast of South America!

My first time experiencing a comment from someone about my dad's music was on YouTube. He was from Sweden. That blew my mind! After that, I received personal emails from Jones' fans living in Italy, Scotland, France, Wales and Germany.

I viewed over the Internet more than once a Jamaican radio station that played Blues Boy Jones' records.

Other places people were listening to his music...Greece, Switzerland, Trinidad & Tabago, Africa, Aruba and many more.

Just think about the places we are not aware of. Yet, people are jamming to these timeless songs that have been around now 60+ years!

The love and respect for my father's legacy seemed endless. And I love it!

His music lives on in the hearts of many generations...

And I graciously with kindness thank EVERYONE for their support!

Please log onto YouTube. Enjoy sharing and viewing Jones' 10 songs.

It was in October 2007, that we discovered "Louis Jones and His Band" mentioned in a story about a music producer, the late Don Robey, also, the owner of Duke-Peacock records, then located in Houston, Texas. My father's song "Rock n Roll Bells" was listed in the company's archives. A picture was discovered in the Duke Peacock records archives at the University of Houston Special Collections Division some eight years later, October 2015.

Jones' music and legacy has gone from unknown to known worldwide, including a photo that was marked "unknown" many years ago!

LOVE, PEACE & MUSIC!

To the Family:

Dad your spirit, your gift of music and your legacy will live on. You are not forgotten! I love and honor you for a lifetime. My mother, nothing can compare to all the love and sacrifices you gave to your family. My love for you is priceless...My brothers Marty James Jones (deceased), Harold Leonard Jones (deceased) and Louis Jones III (now deceased, our family chain was broken once again, my dear oldest brother lost his battle to cancer on December 21, 2014 and life for us will never be the same), sisters Thyra Ann Turk, Pamela Ruth Anderson, Taneshia Aaron Chenier, my children, grandchildren, other family members and friends, you all have brought so much joy to my life, endlessly...I love each of you.

More Family Treasures...

My oldest daughter LaRoysha M.
Jackson Walker R. N. (in the
middle) and her three daughters,
Jaelah M. Jackson now age 18,
Briah L. Walker now age 16 and
Rylee J. Walker now age 8.

My youngest daughter, Minister
Roylisha M. Jackson.

Roylisha's daughter Haven Mo'Nae
Rebecca Jackson, now age 7.

My youngest sister, Taneshia C. Aaron Chenier (Blues Boy Louis' youngest daughter) and her family on her wedding day January, 13, 2012. Her husband Charles S. Chenier, her oldest son Adrien A. Henry and her youngest son Wilajon S. Trail. Taneshia's mother is Lois Marie Thibodeaux.

Andrew Phillip Johnson Sr., now age 90 (Blues Boy Jones' oldest and only living sibling). Jones had only one sister, Laura Mae O'Neal (deceased) and a younger brother Herman Wright Sr. (deceased).

Rebecca Prince Jackson, my Dad's beloved Mom, known to us as Grama. She was the matriarch of our family. She is greatly loved and missed by all of us.

To my family and friends: My journey was smoother because of you. I could never pay any of you enough for all the love and support you gave to me to help make this book possible. I am grateful and blessed to have each of you in my life. A special thank you to all those who made contributions: Kim/Chris Moses Sr., LaRoysha/Bryan Walker, Olivia Stredic, Harold Jones, Jen Johnson, Pastor Hollis O. Lemons and Deacon James T. Bankston Sr. Shout out to the best editors in Texas! (According to me): Minister Roylisha Jackson, Alan Johnson and other editors unspoken.

I cannot express or tell everyone associated with Jones' music and his legacy all of the gratitude that I have in my heart for each of you. No doubt in my mind that Jones' music is internationally known. His music is being enjoyed by people from many generations from the early 1950s up until now. What a blessing and an honor for my Dad! This has been a thrill of a lifetime for me. One of life's greatest treasures is making new friends. I have enjoyed communicating with everybody in places around the globe! On behalf of Blues Boy Jones' legacy and his music, thank you. This has been a great privilege for me and I do not take anything for granted. I thank each person for caring, supporting, listening, sharing and most of all LOVING my dad, the legendary Louis Blues Boy Jones! Gone but never to be forgotten. I thank you all with a smile in my heart...

LaVern Jones Lemons...Author

I want to speak about love, joy, peace and music. In life, love matters the most. No love, no life. Therefore, to me love is like carrying a daily survival kit around with you. Choose to love. Joy lasts longer than happiness. Happiness can be at times something momentary. True joy from deep within the heart, mind and soul will certainly help you enJOY life to the fullest and surely there will be less time for one to stress. I would rather have peace. It gives any situation in life a sense of balance and one will tend worry a lot less. Again, give me peace of mind, peace in my heart, body and my soul! As a little girl I felt in my heart there was just something tremendously special about my dad; now I know why. LOUIS (BLUES BOY) JONES, I will forever love and miss you. Gone but, Daddy I thank you from my heart because you shared the gift of love through your music. The music you left behind is still touching lives in places all around this universe! So be it on a small or large scale, make sure you share your gifts through…Love, Joy, Peace and MUSIC!

God bless all…Forever in my ♥

REAL TALK: One of my biggest joys, is watching my children and grandchildren singing their grandfather and great grandfather's music. For me it is sheer entertainment that's hard to beat. Such a lovely sight to witness and hear!

With all honesty. For this family and myself. We hope one day that someone will come forth concerning the rights to Louis Prince Jones Jr.' music.

YES! I would love to see footage of my Dad on stage...all things are possible...believing.

Expressions of Gratitude:

My deepest gratitude is to a much higher and a spiritual power. First and foremost, God, I thank you for allowing me the opportunity to exist and then for giving me the knowledge to express my thoughts. Dear God, with humility, I thank you.

Although, my father is no longer here, Dad, I thank you from my loving heart. You gave us your very best. My life was spiraling down and I was sad. I needed answers after searching many years and still getting negative feedback about your music. After finding out that people still care, love and respect your music in places worldwide, my life will never be the same.

Because of Jones' many dedicated followers near and far, my loving family and friends, my thanks to each of you are endless. We have to thank the music industry for recognizing my father's talents during his years in the music business. I feel like I am on top of the world!

It has been my pleasure corresponding with many great people all around this big beautiful world via the Internet, telephone calls and personal visits. Although this may seem small to some, the recognition of my father's music and legacy by his followers near and abroad is grander than grand for me. I know for a fact, that everyone associated with Jones' career past or present are definitely the reasons his legacy still lives on today. I get emotional about the love and respect each of you has shown for my father.

I still have work to do. My siblings and I are still seeking to have ownership of our dad's music. People are working in the process to have his music re-issued on a CD.

We hope your hearts are filled with joy as each of you travels down memory lane through the life and times of a blues legend. Hopefully, someone will make a movie or documentary about Jones' life.

The Timeless Music of

LOUIS "BLUES BOY" JONES

Blues Around the World!

Jones was lead vocalist of two bands: Louis Jones and His Band and Louis Blues Boy Jones and the Bobby Scott Orchestra.

1. Rock n Roll Bells

2. All Over Goodbye

3. I'll be Your Fool

4. Someway Somewhere

5. Come on Home

6. I Cried

7. I Believe to my Soul

8. Hurry Baby

9. The Birds is Coming

10. That's Cuz I Love You

Louis Prince Jones Jr.

A must share (Oscar-winning) message of love. People all around the world please read. Thanks with love and gratitude beyond measure to my lil' sister Taneshia...in my eyes you are more than AWESOME! God bless you! A Message from Taneshia Aaron Chenier Feb. 14, 2016:

Hey Big Sister, I don't know what it is about today because you know I don't make Comments on these sites, but today I feel I must make an exception. I want to let you know I am so PROUD of you and I know Dad is SMILING! I PRAY that the GOOD LORD continue BLESSING YOU and DIRECTING YOUR PATH. Who would have thought that by me contacting you years ago about Dad's music STILL being sold on the Internet and people asking me questions about Dad that I could not answer, because I was too young to know anything, would have led to this. I'm saying this to say you have ALWAYS had the TOOL(S) KNOWLEDGE/TALENT etc...but GOD ALLOWED you to use it when it was YOUR SEASON. You see, WE can't do things on OUR time. WE have to do it when GOD LEAD US 'cause if you think back to when I first brought this information to your attention about our dad, you told me you had been wanting to write a book about dad's life for years, but you hadn't started. I guess

OBSTACLES/ QUESTIONS were HINDERING you from making a move. (REMEMBER) Every time we would talk on the phone, I would ask you if you started the book and you would laugh and say, "NOT YET, SIS." Then I would Laugh and reply, "GIRL WHATCHA WAITING ON!" Then ONE BLESSED DAY YOU TOOK A LEAP OUT ON FAITH! PRAISE GOD! And ever since that day, EVERYTHING HAS JUST BEEN FALLING INTO PLACE and I'M OVERWHELMED WITH JOY BECAUSE OF YOUR ACCOMPLISHMENTS and SUCCESS. WITH THAT BEING SAID, HERE'S A PHONE TOAST FROM ME TO YOU. THIS TOAST IS FOR YOUR ACCOMPLISHMENTS/SUCCESS and THIS TOAST IS FOR USING THOSE MANY OBSTACLES AS STEPPING STONES. I LOVE YOU, From your 'lil' Sister, Taneshia